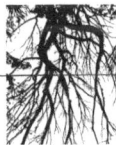

Roots & Branches Series

The Duncan Era

One Reader's Cosmology

Patrick James Dunagan

SPUYTEN DUYVIL
New York City

Library of Congress Cataloging-in-Publication Data applied for

Library of Congress Cataloging-in-Publication Data

Names: Dunagan, Patrick James, author.
Title: The Duncan era : one reader 's cosmology / Patrick James Dunagan.
Description: New York City : Spuyten Duyvil, 2016. | Includes bibliographical
    references.
Identifiers: LCCN 2016020291
Subjects: LCSH: Duncan, Robert, 1919-1988--Criticism and interpretation. |
    Duncan, Robert, 1919-1988. | Poets, American--20th century--Biography.
Classification: LCC PS3507.U629 Z65 2016 | DDC 811/.54--dc23
LC record available at https://lccn.loc.gov/2016020291

CONTENTS

PREFACE

With this essay I've sought to gather together and record my personal responses to various recently published works concerning the magisterial San Francisco poet and thinker Robert Duncan. The University of California Press publication of Duncan's multivolume Collected Works remains a preoccupation throughout. In addition, along with opening chapters concerning Duncan's close poet-peers Robin Blaser and Jack Spicer, numerous recent critical responses to his life and work are engaged.

Attention is given first and foremost to framing a running discussion circling round Duncan's envisioning of his life practice being one of a mirrored experience of the two activities of reading and writing wherein each usurps the other's predilections and predominance in a continual realignment of priority. Such a practice indeed continues to serve as my own guide to understanding the work at hand. By no means has it been my intention to create a work identifiably scholarly in tone or merit. And discipleship is not my game. Nor is this a creative rejoinder, though the Epilogue is decidedly imaginary.

Finally, this is no poet's book of criticism any more than it is an academic endeavor. It is simply a reader's essay written in order that I may further read. That it is in my reading I have discovered my own writing. I offer it in the hope that others may likewise take joy where I myself have most often found it at work in the work.

Patrick James Dunagan
San Francisco
June 27, 2016

When the art is one of reading writing,
     there must be a gramarye kept in which
     the old oracular voice returns

to take over   the poet's intention
     we cannot fathom,   his heart
     in his mouth,   tongue's root

in truth sprung.

     Robert Duncan,
          "Secondary Is the Grammar", *Dante Études*

CHAPTER ONE
OF ROBIN BLASER

Robin reached a point in the poem that I remember as "the voice of the 26 letters thunders in the alphabet and the diaphanous heart is at the door" — and wham! both doors burst open, and the wind or winds die down, and that's it. The curtains stop swaying, the wind's all done with. Then the end of the poem. Then the bluebird song, played twice, and the end of the night. After all that I walked on stage and in the audience buzz of the aftermath told Robin what happened, and he had no idea. "Both doors?" he asked me. "Well, that would be Robert and Jack!! Oh, how I love to conjure spirits when I read."

—Steve Dickison,
"Visitation by Divination: A Ghost Story"

The above epigraph is drawn from a piece that readily demonstrates San Francisco State Poetry Center director and poet Steve Dickison's reverence for poet Robin Blaser's profoundly recognizant awareness of his role in the three-way of poetry which proved central to Blaser's own life. It is a reverence I deeply share.

Blaser's presence in American Poetry often gets overlooked amongst his contemporaries of the divergent "schools" popularly celebrated in Don Allen's now widely-recognized-as-seminal anthology *New American Poetry: 1945-60* (Grove Press 1960). Like so many others, his work straddles the arbitrary divisions Allen sets up in his Introduction. Working as a librarian at San Francisco State, Blaser was a key member of the inner circle within the San Francisco

Renaissance. Although much of this "school" is usually eclipsed by the inclusion of the San Francisco Beats, with the starring event being Allen Ginsberg's landmark 1955 reading of Howl, it was in fact predated and manifestly informed by the earlier Berkeley Renaissance in the late 1940s during Blaser's student years alongside the likes of poets Robert Duncan, Jack Spicer, and William Everson under the semi-led direction of the unofficial grand impresario of the Bay Area poetry scene Kenneth Rexroth.

Despite Blaser's strong ties to San Francisco he also formed deeply lasting connections with the work of poet Charles Olson, the arch-patriarch of the poetics associated with Black Mountain College in North Carolina. In addition, Blaser spent significant time in Boston during the 1950s, a period of fertile development in what has been referred to by poet Gerrit Lansing as the Boston Occult School of Poetry. Other poets sharing similar crossover between San Francisco, Black Mountain, and Boston at the same time include Joe Dunn, John Wieners and Jack Spicer. In Boston, the poet with whom they formed a lasting nexus was Stephen Jonas. This 1950s era Boston gathering, again with deep ties to Olson who was for significant stretches of time living in nearby Gloucester, has proved endlessly influential upon the work of poets such as Gerrit Lansing, Joseph Torra, and Ammiel Alcalay.

After Boston, Blaser returned to San Francisco and later permanently decamped northward to Vancouver in the 1960s taking up a teaching position at Simon Fraser University. However, his place as an American poet is forever sealed by his early experiences in the milieu of these various poetry scenes, particularly in Berkeley and San Francisco where the friendship he shared with Jack Spicer and Robert Duncan is an integral aspect of his lifelong commitment to poetry as an

Order of Craft where one's life is one with one's art. Blaser's steadfast loyalty to his poet-friends and the practice of poetry shared between them couldn't provide starker contrast to today's ever burgeoning dependence upon digital social frameworks for clear instruction of who's in and who's out. As poet Steven Manuel, editor of *from a Compos't*, recently kvetched in an email to me regarding one of the latest bits of poetry world small-time controversies: "The elitist fame-whores vs. the moralizing institution-concerned petitioners. People spend their time doing this instead of reading Plotinus and Robin Blaser." I can't help but feel similarly entrenched alongside Manuel against these abysmal dustups, amazed by the apparently heedless embrace of so many with the muck of our present time, caught up by the latest spiel scrolling down their screens.

Blaser has been on my own mind of late while I've been busily gathering together the disparate pieces of my critical writing from the last few years to form this work about Robert Duncan, which I have entitled *The Duncan Era: One Poet's Cosmology*. Yet the mantle *Era* in the title is equally fitting for each poet of the triumvirate crew forming the actual, true heart of the San Francisco Renaissance: Blaser, Spicer, and Duncan. Three poetiqueers whose mythic association brought such envious yearning into my youthful ideas of the Orders of Imagination, The Poet, and Poetry that I have willingly wagered my own personal relationships on a scale against the example thereby set.

One shouldn't live by one's reading. It is dangerous business to do so, as I have repeatedly learned. Yet nevertheless I pay little heed. For years measuring my own loves, be they personal, poetic, familiar or distant, on a vast stage whereon played out all the loves I admired from the literary works I turned to in my reading, enchanted. In the same spirit, I have always assumed everybody else of interest likewise reads and lives in similar manner. That quite naturally at some future point in time there would be this supernal company I'd find myself amongst as a fellow member, we all equally understandingly appreciating where each one of us stood. Just like it was with Blaser, Duncan, and Spicer ...isn't that how it was for them? ...isn't that how poetry works? Turns out, no, it's not. Not with any purity anyway. This world doesn't recognize any such thing. Nonetheless, I've found a slightly naïve belief in such grand company has been more than enough to carry me through a number of years of self-willed apprenticeship.

Duncan remains the principal abiding concern of this book. I do, however, open with an extensive consideration of Spicer via two recent critical publications concerning his work. Although Blaser may be often left silently in the wings, I could not be more aware of his influence impacting every opinion I offer on both Duncan and Spicer. In any conversation concerning this triumvirate of poets, Blaser should never be forgotten. His work exudes a controlled nuance of effectual displayed poetics placing him between the multi-variable groups within which praise for Duncan and Spicer has found predominant voice. It is delightfully nothing but a pleasure to see *The Astonishment Tapes: Talks on Poetry and Autobiography with Robin Blaser and Friends*, edited by Miriam Nichols, now published (University of Alabama Press 2015). These tapes offer a thorough immersion into the complex idiosyncratic personal nature of poetics practice as well as insight into the Blaser-Duncan-Spicer friendship.

Long heralded yet elusively withheld, the talks comprising *The Astonishment Tapes* occurred during the spring of 1974 over the course of several evenings, referred to as "sessions," in Vancouver at the home of Professor Warren

Tallman. In addition to Tallman as host and mediator of sorts, several local writers were invited to take part in the activities and their presence is reflected to varying degrees. After being stored in a shoebox for decades on a shelf in Tallman's home the tapes have now been digitalized and fully transcribed, totaling "roughly 214,800 words or about 840 manuscript pages." Editor Miriam Nichols has performed an exceptionally difficult task assembling this oversized behemoth of oral document into a quite readable and still satisfyingly expansive published form.

While not the full transcript this selection does cover the complete range of the talks. Nichols has interjected short, informative summaries of whatever material has been skipped over at the point of omission in the text. All omissions appear quite reasonable. In addition, Nichols provides Appendix A: *List of Names*, an enormously useful glossary of who's who in Blaser's lexicon, and Appendix B: *Guide to the Complete Transcription of the Tapes*, equally vital as compensation for the published text's incompleteness. Nichols offers the assurance that "a searchable copy of the full transcript and a digital copy of the audiotapes will be housed in the Contemporary Literature Collection, Simon Fraser University."

At the time of recording the talks, Blaser was in the midst of triumphantly passing on the tremendous legacy of Spicer's poetry and poetics after the latter's early death from alcoholism in 1965. Blaser's life in Vancouver arrived inextricably tied up with Spicer since the position at Simon Fraser was originally offered to Spicer as a result of the popularity of lectures he delivered there, as a guest of Tallman and interested students, in the year before his death. Blaser's editing of *The Collected Books of Jack Spicer* (1975) provided what was to become the classic entry point for nearly every future reader of Spicer over the course of the following decades until appearance of *My vocabulary did this to me: the collected poetry of Jack Spicer* (2008). His defining essay on Spicer's poetics "The Practice of Outside" serves as afterword to *The Collected Books*. It also provides the aforementioned title of *The Collected Poetry*, being literally the poet's dying words spoken directly to Blaser as he memorably relates in the essay's moving closure. In effect Blaser practically launched what might be termed "Spicer studies" under which a significant number of today's younger poets and scholars have made their mark, publishing dozens of essays, along with several dissertations and critical monographs.

The Spicer essay offers previous indication of Blaser's unique style of critical address as a poet-scholar deeply immersed in the poetic alongside dense theoretical texts which he proves ever capable of effortlessly weaving into a learned yet decidedly creative discussion. This same unique style shows itself throughout the talks gathered in *The Astonishment Tapes* where Blaser conducts himself with an intimacy that's by turns profound, hilarious, studied, and provocative. The results are often as much direct as they are obtuse. Occurring when Blaser is midway through his life, these talks are neither introduction nor a summing up; instead they are an immersion into his poetic process in medias res, as it were, granting invaluable insight into his past experience and ongoing practice as creative artist and thinker. As Nichols states, "In my view, these talks are processive rather than magisterial: Blaser works through and toward a language for that story of [his] poetics." That is to say, Blaser reveals the active nature of his own creative method, not only for poetry but life itself.

Nichols describes how "The tapes were meant to be autobiographical, but Blaser did not think of his autobiography as separate from his life as a poet, and he was fierce on this point." There was no singular linear timeline Blaser held himself to as he went through the sessions. Recitation of any one event leads Blaser forward and/or backward, looping up time and again in the endless continual cycle of correspondence within which he lived. Nichols notes: "Readers will notice much repetition; Blaser would think of this as "folding": content from one story is repeated in another context that alters and extends the original content." As Blaser claims in the opening session "I am after folds and want things to layer and fold over one another all the time" revealing his hoped for goal "to make it a conversation in such a way that one could make these folds begin to work." Rather than delivering a straight forward narrative Blaser offers a series of exploratory anecdotal memories of his personal life and creative intellectual development along with key texts upon which he ruminates.

Quotations and allusions to writing by various authors appear strewn through Blaser's poetry, appearing hopelessly immersed amongst the poet's own words, imbuing each text with ethereality beyond the meta-textual. In a similar manner during these talks Blaser frequently moves from one period of time to comment upon another, very much engaging with his life as in a poem: the talks thus becoming an ever expanding instant of creation. Nichols identifies "the major themes—family stories, Spicer and Duncan, [Ernst] Kantorowicz [professor of medieval history at Berkeley], Dante, the metaphysics of light, Joycean modernism, Berkeley poetry wars" which appear. These "might have eventually come together in a narrative of Blaser's own poetics" if only the talks were not incomplete, as "the tapes were abandoned." But completion of a cohesive dramatic overview of his life and work was never what Blaser was after.

Unlike his essay writing, which is immaculately polished, cohesive in tone and structure, Blaser's expressions here are found at times rather raw and unpolished. Blaser did not go over these transcriptions and Nichols keeps any direct editorial changes to a minimum, removing such things as conversational pauses and utterances (e.g. ums and ahs, yeahs and rights). Several strands of thought or points of reference come up only to quickly vanish and never reappear. For instance, at one point when Blaser briefly alludes to several references as coming up in later sessions Nichols explains in a footnote: "Blaser never gets to [Theodor] Adorno's *Negative Dialectics* on these tapes, nor does he give a session on Avicenna, Ibn 'Arabî, or Rumi as he promises a few lines later."

Alternately, Blaser recalls particular memories on multiple occasions in varying form. One of these instances focuses upon key differences he sees between the approaches towards having a relationship with poetry as taken by Duncan and Spicer. The first appearance is during Session 3 (the "it" mentioned here is poetry):

> Duncan says, "I would kick it in the teeth, I wouldn't give anything for it." Jack says, "I'll die if it will speak to me." Jack becomes the lover of the other. Duncan says, "I *am* the other! I speak it!"

This same difference of approach taken by his two closest poet-peers is restated during Session 8. Blaser recalls: "When Duncan was here at Simon Fraser for a reading he said, "I've given nothing up for poetry." This is in contrast—you heard that, Warren—to the cost for people like Jack." Tallman responds: "Well, Duncan once said, "I would kick poetry in the teeth." And Blaser retorts: "Yes, I would kick poetry in the teeth rather than have it cost me." Well worth noting is that in both instances, Duncan is never referred to as "Robert" while Spicer is always referred to as "Jack."

Blaser's personal recollections and critical engagements with the work of Duncan and Spicer assume a central role in the talks. His amusing account—another instance of him repeating himself, he describes the occasion more than once—of his first encounter with Spicer paints an indelible image:

> it's either late-August or early-September '45 when the doorbell rings, 2520 Ridge Road, [Berkeley, CA] and I open the door and there is a mysterious man with a mustache, dark glasses, a trench coat, sandals, his feet painted purple for some incredible reason—it turned out later that it was purple gentian for athlete's foot—and an umbrella, and it's Jack Spicer. He so horrified me in the shadow of that hallway that I slammed the door in his face.

As Blaser articulates the position he maintains in respect to these two poet-peers so central to his life and work, it's clear that his relationship towards Duncan is by far the more contentious. Spicer's death, and Blaser's role as literary executor and steward, has smoothed over any tensions which existed between them as poets and friends. Duncan, however, is far from dead at the time, and had recently publicly castigated Blaser over a difference of poetic opinion concerning a translation of Nerval. As a result, Blaser is consistently forced to assert his independence from Duncan's pervasively willful compulsion towards maintaining control and the upper hand in both friendship and poetry.

Blaser compares his relationship with Duncan to the one he enjoyed with Charles Olson, pinpointing an area of his critique of Duncan while maintaining his utter allegiance to both poets:

One thing I knew about the difference between my relationship with Olson and my relationship with Duncan—two very powerful men whose work was well beyond any range that my work then had, whose thought had moved in a range that I wished to be companion rather than anything else at that point and so on—I knew that Duncan was imposing it on me, and I knew that Olson was composing, and the fearsomeness of Olson was how do you join the composition. With Duncan, it was not that—all you had to do was be a good audience, an intelligent one, and I was. I remain among the best of his audience, if not the most knowledgeable about his work— as far as I know more knowledgeable than anybody who has written, anyway—which is a difference between imposition of content and composition of content.

Blaser moves delicately, yet ever stridently, not so much in opposition to Duncan as searching after means for declaring his independence from him. In the Blaser-Duncan-Spicer poet trio, Blaser is in many ways the late bloomer. *The Astonishment Tapes* has moments of feeling as if it is the tail-end of his emergence from the cocoon of the friendship. (The vast majority of his poetry and essays appeared after these talks were recorded.) Blaser is announcing, even if just to himself in part, that he's through standing in the shadow of his friendships.

At the beginning of the 9th session, Blaser opens with some of the off-the-cuff urbane wit and ever gracious charm he's so well known for: "on the way over here, it's such a quiet day, I opened both windows in the car and a gust of wind came and blew my notes out the window."

Warren questioningly reprimands: "you mean you opened the window and threw your notes out." To which Blaser somewhat acquiesces while dovetailing the probable reason for the wind's actions into an elegant analogy:

I think what I wanted to do was throw them out the window because I have had trouble concentrating. But when they went out the window, I felt a little like that famous Chinese poet, the princess. There are no poems. She's supposed to have been a tremendous poet, but she threw all of her poems in the river as she wrote them, and that's a little the way I felt. Anyway, my house is full of peonies and the perfume of the peonies has been disturbing my mind. I went out into the garden to get away from that and the foxglove is taller than I am and it's full of bees and somehow I don't think my notes came up to that, so the wind took them away from me. It was very strange because it's so still today.

At this point Blaser is clearly beginning to show signs of becoming less interested in continuing the sessions. During the very next session agonizing, "I'm also narrating my own narration so that, I mean simultaneously, so that I go nearly crazy." He continues on, noting how "it just became toxic. I couldn't tolerate it, and I was in a state of collapse last week." Here, near the end of the sessions, Blaser clearly foresees the incompleteness of the project. Yet his original goal was perhaps always intentionally rather far out of reach.

The Astonishment Tapes provide further evidence of how much there is to learn from the Blaser-Duncan-Spicer friendship for any practicing poet. Blaser's reflections reflect the dense thicketed nature of how one's reading writing merges with one's living.

Dickison notes in the closing of his Blaser remembrance, "I keep misreading / misremembering that line of Robert Duncan's as 'an eternal conversation folded in all thought' —that 'pasture' that is 'a meadow' and 'the field.'" How remarkable a notation, for it is only within "conversation" alone that the work of Place is found wherein each poet arrives in a manner which uniquely suits the work itself.

Certainly all of my writing is my own effort to join in celebrating such characteristic engagement between one's life and art. I also hope to perhaps introduce other poets and readers to the abiding importance of what I've found in my own reading. Above all, I heartily encourage that one's writing be one with one's reading, as too one's living, each to each, spurring the other on. I am ever intent on providing example of my strident faith in such practice. I don't believe there's any other path towards poetry.

CHAPTER TWO
THE HAZARDS OF JACK SPICER

I first encountered the poems of Jack Spicer as an undergraduate student at New England College in New Hampshire when I read *The Postmoderns: The New American Poetry Revised* (Grove Weidenfeld 1982) the revised and updated edition of Don Allen's anthology *New American Poetry: 1945-1960* (Grove Press 1960; U.C. Press 1999) however Spicer's work didn't immediately strike my fancy at the time. That wasn't to happen until some years later while browsing among the library shelves at the University of California in Riverside (during a personal furlough of sorts through some definite Purgatory landscape) when I came across *The Collected Books of Jack Spicer* (Black Sparrow Press 1975) edited, after Spicer's early death, by his fellow poet and pal Robin Blaser.

Standing in the aisle puzzling over the first "book" therein, *After Lorca*, with its Introduction clearly written by the ghost (huh?) of the dead poet Federico Garcia Lorca, I first caught glimmerings of how vital Spicer's work would prove to be in relation to my own concerns as a poet, playing a major role in my conceptions surrounding poetry. At the time I was looking ahead to graduate school in Poetics at New College in San Francisco and attempting to prepare myself for future study by becoming familiar with all things poetry, most especially concerning those poets whose work immediately appealed to me. In terms of my own reading habits, this has always entailed performing what poet Charles Olson refers to as a "saturation job" of reading EVERYTHING available on any given figure of interest. With Spicer in Riverside, this resulted in my soon finding the back issues of *Boundary 2* wherein, among numerous other delights, was the Spicer issue (bound together with the Dickinson issue, portraits of each poet adorning the respective cover) chock full of essays on the work along with his "plan for a book of Tarot."

Within a year I was in San Francisco walking the same streets Spicer had some four decades previous, visiting the same and/or similar North Beach drinking establishments, arguing, cajoling, his poems spilling round in my head. Soon thereafter Kevin Killian and Lewis Ellingham's Spicer biography *Poet Be Like God* (Wesleyan University Press 1998) appeared, almost immediately Spicer's name started to emerge more and more in classes, bar conversations, and during poetry readings. Poetryworld was quickly discovering, or re-discovering as the case were, the fantastic nooks and crannies of Spicer's poetic realm filled with his Martians, Spooks, Ghosts, Billy the Kid, baseball, pinball machines, Lorca, and Cocteau imagery.

For a short period of time it remained possible to find on the shelf at neighborhood bookstores cheap used copies of *The Collected Books*, the odd Spicer issue of an earlier magazine, such as *Manroot* (no. 10, Fall 1974/Win 1975), or the collection with the lengthily weighted introduction by Robert Duncan *One Night Stand and Other Poems* (Grey Fox Press 1980). The latter being a comprehensive gathering of the predominately early, solitary Spicer poems not organized into sequential book-length sets of series he came to favor in his mature output and which Blaser honored in his editing of *The Collected Books*.

Joining in with *Poet be Like God's* interjection of Spicer with a thundering force into the heart of poetryworld discourse, Peter Gizzi's *The House that Jack Built: the collected lectures of Jack Spicer* (Wesleyan 1998) further contributed to encouraging the ongoing drone of Spicerian poems, homages, accolades, and inevitable dissertations (Gizzi's book of the lectures is in fact his own dissertation).

I began to hear that Killian and Gizzi had students at work on going through the Spicer archive gathering potential material for a larger *Collected Poems*, perhaps part of a projected multi-volume set of Spicer material to appear from Wesleyan (publisher of both the biography and lectures). *My Vocabulary Did this to Me: the Collected Poetry of Jack Spicer* (Wesleyan 2008) has since appeared and various murmurings over the years indicate there may very well be at least one or two further volumes to appear: a collection of Spicer's correspondence and/or yet still more poems together with some plays. In 2011, Wesleyan kept the attention-pot stirred, releasing *After Spicer: Critical Essays* edited by John Emil Vincent. For better or worse, Spicer is now worked into the academic labor mill as far as nearly any poet of his generation.

Critical perspectives on Spicer such as Daniel Katz's *The Poetry of Jack Spicer* (Edinburgh University Press 2013) and those gathered in Vincent's *After Spicer* at first nearly seem more belated than anything. As Vincent reminds us, Spicer "is now considered one of the major forebears of the Language movement, and has become what his biographers call a 'cult figure.'" Spicer's "notorious crankiness" as both bad boy and precursor-figure to post-modern American poetry is quickly gaining recognition across diverse international poetry communities. I have heard that even his more obscure text "Unvert Manifesto" has been translated into Farsi among underground poets in Iran. The attention increasingly continues appear in rather unlikely contexts. Spicer's work arises from a self-imposed, unresolvable dilemma of dueling characteristics; the gleeful game of bait-and-switch, the send-ups and take-downs of both opposition figures and scenes, those fictional as well as factual.

Katz's book-length critical study is the only one existing which consists of a complete overview of Spicer's body of work. Katz proves himself eminently up for the task. There's little within Spicer criticism of which he does not manage to at least touch upon. Katz accomplishes a thorough introduction that is at once also not lacking in fresh insight. The bar is set high for future would-be Spicer critics and scholars. While the focus throughout remains scholarly Katz's general tone tends towards the conversational (with only occasional brief slides into academic jargon) and he does a highly efficient job filling in biographical detail without besotting his critical lens with heavy quoting of sources or random listing of facts. The result is an impressive condensing of a large amount of information, the offered judgment of which is all spot on.

No matter the approach taken to his work Spicer remains both purposively elusive and delightfully enchanting. In her contribution to Vincent's book, "Character Assassination in the Poetry of Jack Spicer," Anita Sokolsky frames it up nicely: "Spicer's distinctiveness as a poet might be said to derive from his relentlessly equivocal relation to the premises of a language poetry of which he is being currently reclaimed as a founder. His work adamantly refuses to be the progenitor of any poetic line." In fact, the inherent de-centering nature of his work ensures the great irony that as Spicer is accepted and studied, within and by "the poetry establishment," in any and all senses of that term, even as his work continues identifying itself in opposition to such acceptance

Katz's book at times serves more as an introductory overview rather than as engaging original criticism in its own right. He fails explore some areas. This is usually due to the fact that he resists embracing elements of Spicerian lore choosing rather to stick with the nuts and bolts of Spicer's poetics. He makes no mention of Spicer's interest in the

Tarot, for instance. There is also little discussion of Spicer's bioregional interests, his San Francisco-centric ideals get only passing reference—readers are directed elsewhere in footnotes.

Yet when read as a gay man, as his work generally insists upon, Spicer's poetics become only further complicated. Included by Vincent, Catherine Imbriglio's "'Impossible Audiences': Camp, the Orphic, and Art as Entertainment in Jack Spicer's Poetry," tackles the question of Spicer's Orphic use of and alignment within and against camp:

> surface and depth, real and imaginary—all of which are complexly aligned and misaligned in Spicer's Orphic/ camp relations—press a double sense of frustration and groundlessness onto the "Love Poems" once camp and Orphic border crossings and related dismantlings are entertained. Paradoxically, it is the poet as poet and camp performer who willfully activates the attempts at border crossings and related dismantlings that result in the terrifying sense of groundlessness, frustration, and near disintegration.

In a Spicer poem, words are transformed in meaning, while simultaneously exalted for whatever qualities held beforehand, as they are put to use for and against each other. Spicer consistently plays everything as many ways as possible.

In addition, Kevin Killian's contribution to the Vincent book focuses on Spicer's 1953 involvement with the early gay liberation organization Mattachine Society and fills in a heretofore unannounced blank spot in *Poet Be Like God*. Drawing upon previously unavailable historical records containing the official Minutes from group meetings, Killian's narrative is at once eye-opening and confirms assertions concerning Spicer's duality and self-satisfying inclination towards contradictoriness.

[Spicer] used his teenage confusion to argue that bisexuality should be maintained as long as possible, while Gerald Brisette and others maintained that a gay man should come out, at least to himself, at the very first opportunity. For Spicer, it seems, ripeness was all. "That's stirring and all that, Jerry," he drawled, "but say a kid, seventeen, attracted to both men and women…if he makes this decision [that he's gay] at seventeen, he's shutting himself off to half of experience. That's no good." A shout of protest went up, but Spicer continued to play choice as overrated. "If he cut off his balls, that's a choice, too. Why [then make] a choice? Here's an example, 'I'm not going to sleep with Republicans any more. Or Democrats.' Good. Forward moving. Show maturity." Spicer's heavy sarcasm was sometimes a topic killer, but often enough it propelled a discussion along new avenues. Here he pretends to be open to everything, but if there was anyone in the Mattachine who could draw an uncrossable line in the sand, it was Jack Spicer. He was comfortable as a contrarian, the joker in the pack, even when his own irony forced him into a corner, on his own in the middle of a crowd.

Maintaining a position of impossible meeting, the imbalanced act of holding art and life irretrievably tangled, allows Spicer to question any notion of fixed reality by way of mixing it with that of the creative act. This holds an inexhaustible allure for him that his work ceaselessly explores.

Throughout his study Katz seems intent more on reading Spicer less as a California poet consumed by his own personal occult world in favor of just generally as a poet. He also makes no mention of the California poet Robinson Jeffers, whom Gizzi handily draws upon showing several corollaries with Spicer in his afterword to the *Lectures*. There's no cause to feel that Katz is intentionally side-lining the occult or the politics of the local from Spicerian scholarship, only that these interests did not find a place within his own tackling of Spicer as a subject. Certainly there are frequent openings where Katz leaves opportunity for further scholarship to explore these and other areas. At no point does it feel as if he's refusing their relevance.

In his Coda, Katz describes how in the late 1950s Spicer rather surprisingly began "compiling a manuscript for a projected 'selected poems,'" he goes on, detailing this unlikely seeming enterprise:

> ...many of the poems from *A Book of Music* figure in it. This means that well after the rousing letter to Blaser in *Admonitions* excoriating the individual lyric, Spicer was still seriously putting together a collection of them, and refusing to abandon a project whose inadequacy he himself had so passionately argued. One has to imagine that an ultimate commitment to the "book," perhaps solidified by *Billy The Kid*, is what prevented the "selected poems" from ever seeing the light of day, but in the wake of *Admonitions* it's hard to see how Spicer could have continued to work on such a project without serious misgivings and a bad sense of faith.

It's also possible that such a gathering on Spicer's part was very much a competitive gut reaction to publication of his pal Robert Duncan's own *Selected Poems* by City Lights which appeared in 1959. Either way, the fact that Spicer ever assembled such a manuscript does extend as well as complicate the poet-figure with which so much of Spicer lore has left emblazoned in the imagination.

Katz quotes the following unpublished poem, titled "Poet" or "A Portrait", which Spicer placed at the end of this "selected poems."

> He knocks upon our doors un-
> Cannily

As if the only test
Were some way of being right
That a poem can give one

A clear moment of The Poem announcing that The Poet in fact at the time of writing is but somewhat hapless observer to subsequent events. It is also simultaneously rather hair-raisingly reminiscent of the Spicer poet peer with whom his work shares the borrowing of Cowboy Western motifs along with a bitingly humorous sardonic outlook, namely the poet Ed Dorn. The first appearance of the title character central to Dorn's later epic *Gunslinger* occurs in Dorn's "An idle visitation" wherein those "slender leather encased hands / folded casually / to make his knock, / will show you his map. / There is your domain."

Although Dorn's poem is written nearly a decade later, while he's in residence in England, he was in fact living in San Francisco during the later 1950s. Spicer had already written *Billy the Kid* and he went on to write the only latterly discovered "Map Poems." It's alluring to attempt hear in this "lost to the archive" poem a distant echo of what might just be the conversation "in the air" round North Beach bars of the 1950s having filtered its way from Spicer's lips to Dorn's ear, eventually laying some elemental features within the grid-work upon which *Gunslinger* would partly work out its formation.

There's no doubting that the social poetry scene played an integral working role across Spicer's own oeuvre. Another work in Vincent's collection Kelly Holt's "Spicer's Poetic Correspondence" maps out the intricacies of correspondence within which Spicer imbedded his writing, drawing upon his time at U.C. Berkeley when along with Blaser and Duncan he was studying under the medievalist historian Ernst Kantorowicz: "With Kantorowicz, Spicer studied Petrarch's letters to Cicero as an exemplary correspondence between the living poet and his simultaneous *auctor* (author) and *authoritas* (author-text). His correspondence composed a stylistic connection of rhetorical eloquence as a direct address through *epistolae*." Spicer held so strongly onto such "correspondence" between the life lived and the life as written, that, as Vincent's own chapter on Spicer's unfinished novel states, "Spicer's novel and his affair with Russell Fitzgerald are inextricably bound with one another." Writing for Spicer was an interrogation of his own love life with others as much any lover's quarrel might hope to be.

One of the more entertaining as well as enlightening contributions to Vincent's book is Michael Snediker's chapter, "Jack Spicer's *Billy The Kid*: Beyond the Singular Personal" which draws attentively upon "Arthur Penn's 1958 film *Left-Handed Gun*, written by Gore Vidal, a film which Spicer biographers claim as one of Spicer's favorites." Billy's gang hides out in a cabin in the film "festooned with Billy's own Wanted posters," as Snediker describes it, "The myriad posters want Billy dead. The deconstructive strain of much early Spicer criticism—not to mention the more practical logic of small-town law—would argue that the posters not only want that death, but portend it." Like the saying goes, the writing is on the wall. Spicer's work finally centers upon the opening to a dead end street as much as Duncan's (or Blaser's for that matter) represents poetry as a quasi-spiritual calling to higher orders. For Spicer there is nothing worth saving.

Spicer's poetry spends a hazardous amount of time entertaining thoughts of ghosts, death, aliens, the various Outside(s) from where he claimed the poems arrive already dictated. This eventually comes to represent a near religious order. A tragic turn for a man whose religious inclinations were detrimental, as Norman Finkelstein's superb contribution to Vincent's gathering "Spicer's Reason to 'Be- / leave'" clearly enunciates, "his Calvinism proves monstrous and inescapable." Spicer placed control over his life in the hands of poetry as one might a faith. He has now become far too often exactly what he was intent on and aware of becoming: material for scholars and poets to argue over.

For a long while the buzz round Spicer has been loud, often approaching the distinct feeling of being a fad. Several elements of the work (overlapping even when at apparent odds with one another) contribute to the likeliness of such a possibility: his homosexuality, his anarchistic point of view, the belatedness of any sort of mainstream publication, the linguistics (which was his 'profession' if he is to be seen as having one) at work/play in his poems, alcoholism, and the deceptively simple seeming breaks of his line often combined with a lightness of colloquial diction. There's much that it's deceptively easy 'to get', process, incorporate, and write back to in response. Indeed, "correspondence" appears as a key device, repeatedly manifesting as both fascination and tool with which Spicer interacts, encouraging endless possible connections indiscriminately merging: past/present/future, imagination/reality, dead/living, magic/science, reader/poet, poem/poet. But in the end, Spicer courts us as he also abuses us. Dangling a dangerous game just within reach, tempting a following that he'd mockingly scorn. Be wary.

CHAPTER THREE
INTO THE MAZE: ROBERT DUNCAN ENCHANTS

Recent years have witnessed an exciting upsurge in posthumous publications by and about San Francisco poet Robert Duncan. Most significantly, in 2011 University of California Press began publication of the long expected multi-volume *Collected Writings of Robert Duncan*. During the same period, among a rather dizzying array of publications, University of Iowa Press put out *Reading Duncan Reading: Robert Duncan and the Poetics of Derivation* (University of Iowa Press 2012) a collection of essays edited by Stephen Collis & Graham Lyons, while in 2013 City Lights re-published an expanded edition of Michael Rumaker's richly-hued memoir *Robert Duncan in San Francisco* (originally published by Donald Allen's Grey Fox press in 1996). The time has never been riper for the opportunity of a Duncan craze to ignite among robust poetry communities from Oakland to Brooklyn and everywhere in between. Of course, the greatest impasse keeping any craze from happening is the work itself. Clocking in at some 800 pages, each volume of the two volume *Collected Poems and Plays* (U.C. Press) demonstrates the massive size of Duncan's oeuvre; often overflowing with arcane esotericism and personal obscurities, yet the richness of poetic lore surrounding his vast output also attests to its essential value.

For many contemporary readers of poetry, there is no easy entrance into Duncan's work. The *Collected Early Poems and Plays* is likely to be found only the more difficult by the fact it covers material pre-dating his well-known and most anthologized works, such as the seemingly ever-parodied yet nonetheless central "Often I am Permitted to Return to

A Meadow" from *The Opening of the Field*. Only one of the essays in *Reading Duncan Reading*, Sarah E. Ehlers' "Robert Duncan's Miltonic Persuasion: The Emergence of a Radical Poetic", even focuses exclusively upon the early work. By all present accounts, today's readers and critics are far more prevalently drawn to Duncan's later poems, however the majority of the *Collected Early,* originally published by small presses and little magazines, has never been readily available until now. Any apparent lack of interest among readers is regrettable as it proves well deserving of greater attention. Duncan is found to be ever versatile as he consistently explores influences building up the enormous range he later draws upon.

There is much to praise in the over-all editing of the *Collected Early.* Duncan did not gather together and publish the vast majority of the material in collections until much later in the 1950s and 1960s. When doing so, as these were often in volumes presented as "Selected Poems" he frequently fiddled around with the texts, adding and removing individual lines as well as individual poems. He also had opportunity to re-publish some collections. *Caesar's Gate,* for instance, was originally published by Robert Creeley's Divers press in 1955 in Mallorca and was subsequently re-published by Sand Dollar press in 1972. Duncan not only added poems, but wrote an extended new Preface, which is thankfully included as an appendix. In addition, original collages for *Caesar's Gate* made by Duncan's life-partner the artist Jess are reproduced as are line-drawings made by Duncan for *Letters.* The lengthy selection of appendixes and notes to individual poems and volumes, make it possible to track Duncan's various alterations as he published and re-published them, and also provide testament to the fact of how serious and committed a poet Duncan was at the earliest of stages.

Duncan's confidence in his own nature came early and he was ever strident in holding himself to his beliefs. He was an outspoken gay man when there was absolutely no acknowledgement, let alone awareness of, such a concept as gay rights (see his article "The Homosexual in Society" published in *Politics* March 1944). His poems refuse to pass over or hide the gender of the beloved. His radical culturally-innovative stance infamously led to *Kenyon Review* editor John Crowe Ransom first accepting and then rejecting Duncan's poem "An African Elegy" after publication of Duncan's groundbreaking essay. Michael Rumaker is one of the rare first hand chronicles of the pre-Stonewall era of gay culture. Writing from within the extreme homosexual taboo of the time, Rumaker's *Robert Duncan in San Francisco* is a one-of-a-kind glimpse into Duncan's life, not so much the individual particulars but more so the over-arching climate of 1950s San Francisco during which Duncan's powers as a poet flourished into maturity.

The earliest poems included in the *Collected Early* were printed in Kern county high school publications of the early 1930s under the name "Robert Symmes" which Duncan's adoptive parents gave him. While the last work included, *Letters*, was written from 1953-1955 when Duncan was in his mid-thirties and deeply involved with poet-editor/publishers of Black Mountain College: Robert Creeley, Charles Olson, Denise Levertov, and Jonathon Williams. In his Introduction to *Reading Duncan Reading*, Stephen Collis notes "much of what is characteristic in Duncan's work derives from his being the sort of poet who *thematizes* poetry itself" and "the issue of derivative authorship that Duncan's practice proposes continues to be of material import." The phenomenal output of the *Collected Early* is demonstrative of the "derivative poetics" Duncan frequently espoused, often speaking of himself as derivative a term which he claimed as a mantle of pride rather than a fault. (For readers interested in reading Duncan's own words on his poetics, North Atlantic Books recently published the quite substantial and indispensable *A Poet's Mind: Collected Interviews with Robert Duncan*.)

Reading Duncan Reading is divided into two groups of essays: "Duncan Reading" and "Reading Duncan." All the essays demonstrate how strongly Duncan's work is tied compositionally to his reading and other interaction with the work of fellow poets. Moving from a demonstration of his own declared derivations (found within the work itself) from Milton and the English Metaphysical Poets to Laura Riding, Pound, Olson and Zukofsky, on to explorations of inter-connections his work shares with contemporaries and younger peers: John Cage, Jerome Rothenberg, Nathaniel Mackey, Susan Howe, and Ronald Johnson. The emphasis throughout is placed upon how text interacts with text. Consciously and not, Duncan's work strives to exist as a point of blurring where aspects of authorship, personality, and homage are intertwined beyond clear recognition. Often intentionally complicated by personal strife, Duncan's work reflects his own dynamic nature.

University of California Press also recently published poet Lisa Jarnot's biography of Duncan *Ambassador from Venus*, which possesses a surprisingly clipped narrative, notably lacking in personal details. For instance, *Reading Duncan Reading* has no less than two essays concerning the relationship between Duncan and poet Ronald Johnson while Jarnot makes no mention of the younger poet whatsoever. So it is a pleasure to find that where Jarnot's book retains a self-proclaimed distance from her subject, Rumaker's memoir offers a vivid description of Duncan right down to juxtaposing his fashion sense with that of his peer San Francisco poet Jack Spicer.

Robert's dress at that time could be described as
"California Poet Casual." Unlike the tight work jeans,
faded blue work shirt, black turtle neck sweater, stevedore
sock hat, high-laced works hoes and leather jacket that
was poet Jack Spicer's only outfit and made him look like
any longshoreman on the Embarcadero, Robert wore full-
sleeved shirts of soft material with broad collars in earth
as well as bright pastel colors. He particularly favored, for
parties and readings, a wide purple tie with the fattest
Windsor knot I'd ever seen. A bright orange tie and a pink
one were also worn, but not as often.

As the relationship between Duncan and Spicer is a
fascinating and complex klausterfokken situation of rival
love mixed within a more than ample generosity of kindred
spirit, Rumaker's descriptions of the poets are invaluably
perfect gems for broadening readers' visualization of their
opposing personalities.

Throughout the *Collected Early* there are repeated
instances where the Duncan/Spicer friendship is attested and
the crosstalk between each of their poetry is on prominent
display. Included are several homages by Duncan to the
Spanish poet Federico Garcia Lorca which predate Spicer's
own book *After Lorca*. In addition, there is Duncan's "Elegy
Written 4-7-53 for Jack Spicer" which describes "the wizard
text of his mind" and the "multitude of moonish mirrors" in
which the poem proposes:

> It is in their contradictions that the images
> exactly resemble the words of the text . . .
> and figure to the imagination appropriate shapes,
> the genesis and Deuteronomy of his mind.
> He himself is a tabula rasa upon which
> daily he scribbles the same
> > torah, laws, chronicles and pother
> > in which panther and lamb lie down together,
> > a veritable book of friendships.

and goes on to declare:

> He has been de-friended to become
> this friend of a poetry, wingd as he never was,
> increased from all veritable fragmentary acquaintance
> into this singular third person invention,
> the jokester's monotheistic mind picturing
> himself as a poet unbuilt in man's image.

The wry jokiness of an "elegy" written while the addressee was quite alive (Spicer died in 1965) would certainly not have been lost on the subject himself. Spicer's own textual deaths and representative voices of the dead (Lorca and Billy the Kid) are frequent in his work. For familiar readers, the symbiosis in play within the friendship has never been more evident.

Duncan's poetry friendships began early in his life (he mingled with Anaïs Nin's circle in NYC) and reached one notable apex in the later 1940s, during a period often referred to as the Berkeley Renaissance, when Duncan, Spicer, and the poet Robin Blaser first met. This broadened Duncan's already closely knit group of friends bonded by a communal love of books and art. Consequential aspects of this friendship are reflected in Duncan's 'Berkeley Poems" from 1946, particularly "Among my friends love is a great sorrow" with its morosely tinged lines of somber acceptance:

We have become our own realities.
We seek to exhaust our lovelessness.

Among my friends love is painful question.
We seek out among the passing faces
A sphinx-face who will ask its riddle.
Among my friends love is an answer to a question
that has not been askd.
Then ask it.

Among my friends love is a payment.
It is an old debt for a borrowing foolishly spent.
And we go on, borrowing and borrowing
    from each other.
Among my friends love is a wage
that one might have for an honest living.

Duncan's friendship often came with criticism and quarrel. He refused to placate either himself or his friends.

His correspondence is full of instances of challenge and debate as he clashed with views of others, often at the insistence of listening to and following through with his own poetry. Scholar Siobhán Scarry's contribution to *Reading Duncan Reading* details an instance where part of Duncan's later poem "Night Scenes" arose from such a spat in his correspondence. Duncan had sent his book *Letters* to his longtime friend Mary Fabili, with whom he had recently been back in touch after her conversion to Catholicism. She in turn not only found Duncan's work "overly derivative of Stein and Pound" but, as Scarry describes, a letter of hers is "forthright in expressing her concern for Duncan's soul." Scarry includes a portion of Fabili's letter and also a complete draft of an unpublished poem "In Perplexity" from Duncan's notebook which he began in response, providing "a raw look into Duncan's thinking on religion, orthodoxy and homosexuality." Scarry goes on to describe how Duncan salvaged the last stanza of this poem in "Night Scenes." This is but one example of how any and all friction in friendship nearly always proved generative for Duncan's own work.

The derivative nature of Duncan's poetic practice embedded itself in every corner of his life. "The Poem" was not only in effect "The Life" but "The World" as well. There was to be no clear separation. The basis of his belief in his own identity, wherein myth and biography are of one in the same nature, clearly refuses it. The newly added letters and interview to Rumaker's memoir reinforce the challenging struggle Duncan's friendship often proved to be. In the final letter to Duncan included, looking back in 1961 on the previous years covered in the memoir, Rumaker begins "I have re-read your letters" announcing "Now I find them filled with kindnesses I cherish. They are dear to me." Only to then immediately admit "But I have always been so troubled by you." Nonetheless, in the interview Rumaker readily acknowledges Duncan in remarkable terms that are at once personal and historically as well as culturally relevant today.

> Obviously he really is a truly great American poet, I have high respect for that certainly . . . on the personal side, which to me was only interesting because it rounded out the picture, we all have our flaws, and I certainly wrote about mine, in Black Mountain Days, or other books, but the main thing is what he accomplished in spite of all *that stuff*. I respected him not only for his genius, and what he did with it, but for his courage at that particular time. He was like one of those beacons, someone to really look forward to, look to and say, well if he can do this so can I. I mean he fed my own gumption to be not destroyed by these homophobes. That's putting it too bluntly, too simply. Not only as a homosexual, but as a writer, as all those things that you were, or are. Duncan didn't get sucked down by that, he didn't get trapped by that.

Back of everything else, the writing for Duncan remained paramount. The writing which was so utterly inseparable from his reading; but not in any selective sense: ALL his reading and writing came together in one locus of momentary being which he then poured into the occasion of the poem underhand. This practice of Duncan's began early in his life and only increased in intensity at an ever constant rate until his death.

Critic Peter O'Leary's contribution to *Reading Duncan Reading* is "Talking Cosmos: Robert Duncan and Ronald Johnson." Towards the end, he cites an introduction Johnson gave for a reading of Duncan's at San Francisco State in 1984 which provides an additional glimpse into what Duncan's friendship meant. Johnson describes Duncan as "one of the two friends I have on this earth who knows everything I want to know, and always gives me more than I imagined." Duncan is likewise generous to readers approaching his work for the first or infinite number of subsequent times. There is always another, unexpected phrasing or concept expressed which somehow proves essential to current concerns. A surprising juxtaposition of images so stridently affirmed in such peculiarly yet strikingly ostentatious manner its validity returns readers to his poetry again and again. To read Robert Duncan is to engage in an all-consuming, never-ending voyage full of political, personal, cosmic, literary, and ultimately unavoidable, ramifications.

CHAPTER FOUR
DUNCAN & JESS: THE IMAGINATION, THE HOUSEHOLD,
FRIENDSHIP, LOVE & ART

The poet Ronald Johnson rather infamously referred to San Francisco as Oz, the Emerald City freely inter-mingling his love of Frank L. Baum's novels about the magical realm with his poeticized vision of the real city in which he lived for a significant period of his adult life from the 1970s up until the early 1990s. His vision of his adopted hometown however was likewise adopted, having earlier been a firmly shared, key connection in the romantic relationship of poet Robert Duncan and the artist Jess. The couple met each other in Berkeley during the 1950s and soon set up a household together in San Francisco (with various relocations from Stinson Beach to Mallorca, with a short stint at Black Mountain College, back to San Francisco) lasting until Duncan's death in 1988. In the 1960s with a small windfall from some family inheritance along with some benefactor assistance and pooling together Duncan's income from poetry reading fees with Jess' gallery sales, they purchased a Victorian House in the Mission district in which they thereafter resided. Baum's novels had their own set of shelves among the many themed-libraries abounding in different rooms throughout their home. In addition to many, many books, art works adorned every wall and surface.

As with another poet-related show *John Ashbery Collects: Poet Among Things* (Loretta Howard Gallery September 12 - November 2, 2013) the items, objects, and art found throughout the household of Duncan and Jess are star features in *An Opening of the Field: Jess, Robert Duncan, and Their Circle*

(Crocker Art Museum June — August 2013). The collection of material assembled together here is a major celebration of their artistic lives where the imagination reigns supreme. In the catalog for the Ashbery show, Adam Fitzgerald notes how Ashbery's "Hudson house has only recently entered into the awareness of a small group of scholars, critics, fellow poets and artists, who are beginning to develop a vocabulary and methodology to assess its significance." In contrast, 3267 20th Street in the Mission district of San Francisco has long been in the sights of Duncan/Jess enthusiasts yet similarly the critical process of assessing "its significance" is just beginning. This show is a fundamental first step as are the accompanying essays in the catalog.

In addition to the many pieces drawn directly from Duncan/Jess's home, two DVDs playing on looped feeds offer unbridled viewing of the interior space of 3267 20th Street itself: Richard O. Moore's WNET *The Originals: The Writer in America—Robert Duncan* contains footage of Duncan walking through several rooms, discussing and reading from his work, while co-curator Christopher Wagstaff's and David Fratto's *The Household of Robert Duncan & Jess: An Intimate Portrait of a Legendary Home* is a 20 minute visual room-by-room, bookshelf-by-bookshelf, artwork-by-artwork walkthrough of the entire house. As Duncan's biographer, Lisa Jarnot, remarks in a recent interview: "in their house you really felt like a participant in the imaginary, in the 'made place;' it was an amazing place to be." When taken as a whole, the entire exhibit affords a previously heretofore unavailable immersion into this "made place", containing an impressively large number of intimate companion-pieces central to both of their individual arts and full of visual cues for further elaborating upon influences evident in their own works.

The majority of the artists and work included date back to the San Francisco area during the 1940s and 1950s. Several of the artists (including Jess) attended either Berkeley and/ or later the California School of Fine Arts/San Francisco Art Institute. Others, such as Paul Alexander and Tom Field followed Duncan in a general westward drift away from the slow disintegration of Black Mountain College in the mid-1950s. Painter Virginia Admiral's connection to Duncan however began in the 1930s and continued during the early 1940s in New York City. Together they stood apart in the social crowd gathered around Anaïs Nin who "observed in her diary, 'They are both children out of *Les Enfants Terribles*.'" There's something entirely fun about thinking of Duncan palling round with the mother of actor Robert De Niro—who also loaned one of the works included in the show. Admiral's paintings are quite pleasing to look at, richly colorful, and fully rewarding in their delivery of a post-Picasso European abstraction. Both of these two fairly large works of hers are easily among the nicest of surprises to be seen.

As noted with Admiral, the work by women in the show is top notch across the board demonstrating the central relevance Duncan and Jess's reverence for female-artist companions played in their day-to-day living. The only cause for disappointment is being left wishing for a great deal more work to be on hand. From balladeer-poet Helen Adam's familiar (to many of her readers, at least) and terrific collage work—the mixed-media studies of the relationship between classic femininity and surreal horror/absurdity sends the head spinning—to the completely satisfying surprise of Madeline Gleason's alternately bright, nightlife filled early paintings to her more broodingly moody "semi-religious" later work; the women writers in Duncan's circle prove themselves as interested and accomplished, if not more so, as Duncan himself in the visual arts. Similarly, Fran Herndon's paintings only further substantiate the artistic strength with which she engaged the often literary-heavy portrayed atmospherics of the San Francisco Renaissance. Herndon's *Jack Spicer and His Radio* is an especially apt companion-painting to the poet's own work, capturing the warmth, along with childlike glee of their relationship. This glee carries over as well into her painting *Opening Day* with its depiction of baseball being played with rabbits in hand rather than balls.

Nemi Frost's portrait paintings likewise offer a fun-hearted glimpse of this social circle of artists that is yet both psychologically and mythically serious. *Portrait of Robert Duncan* doesn't hold back its punches, softly mauling as they may be. Duncan lies on a Freudian-style analysis couch with a look of inert melancholic whimsy as a lion mounts the couch at his feet. Whimsy is also the order of the day in *The Mad Hatter's Tea-party, Starring Dora Dull and Tom Field* where an extra-bulbous looking Field is slathered in a pink and black super-hero-like look and Dull is graciously draped in oranges and browns with one breast exposed, holding a cup aloft resembling some Tarot insignia. Meanwhile Frost's *Aunt and Joss (Whippet)* possesses a fascinating visual texture. The artist has pasted flowery wallpaper to canvas in order to form the dress of the "Aunt" figure in the painting while bold, solid colors of large fronds provide the background. Such strongly dark choices of color mark Frost's work out as explorations of fantastical mirror-realities of the everyday.

Works by Patricia Jordan and Lyn Brockway further round out the social milieu in which these artists intermingled. Brockway's *Breakfast in a Paris Lodging* being a still life from her trip abroad with fellow artist Jay De Feo as newly university graduated young artists in the early 50s. The gravelly partial-spiral turns of paint immediately enchant, offering what is a classic Parisian setting: a corner countertop with steel percolator atop a Bunsen burner and baguette propped up against white-grey wall. Alternately, Jordan's Stinson Beach photographs offer relaxed images of a bearded Jess and Duncan in shorts ready for an afternoon at the beach yet instead cozied up at home with his writing. While an intricate vertical scroll work by Jordan, *Golden Damsels Descending from the Clouds* contains several photos of Shirley Berman, wife of artist Wallace Berman (publisher of *Semina*, some of whose work is included here), looking the ever bohemian, ever chic Goddess of sorts she's remembered as, surrounded by "Byzantine religious icons, Pre-Raphaelite nudes, Egyptian hieroglyphics, Aztec Gods, and Hindu deities" while Jordan's handwritten text taken from Song of Solomon 7:1 runs round its borders.

Among the most startlingly works are sculptures by Miriam Hoffman. A piece such as *Goddess* from 1953 looks forward towards what's at the time yet to come from the California Assemblage works of George Herms (who also has work included here) and Bruce Conner. Apparently discarded materials used include: a short plank of wood, another shorter, smaller scrap of wood, and some bit of scratchy-looking metallic fabric, all of which Hoffman has arranged with a cross-legged ceramic female figurine in attentive prayer-position facing one mid-sized ceramic head placed before her on the plank and a smaller head atop the scrap of wood which is raised up in the position of a leaning podium with one end of the wire wrapped around it and the other end attached to the fabric which clings to the side of sitting figure's head. Hoffman has an apparent fascination with totemic heads. In a fascinating act of doubling-up on implications and images, readily recognizable faces appear directly behind the front "face" of many of her works, as though emerging from out the work, perhaps offering possible alternate directions and intentions. Such duplicate faces, or indeed duplicate heads, appear embedded in the base of the spectacular, impressive in size, *Head*, which unfortunately won't be appearing outside of Sacramento but is deservingly in the permanent collection at Crocker Museum.

The catalog published by Pomegranate Communications (2013) is tremendously useful and necessary in itself marking a lasting contribution to Duncan Studies, particularly the central role visual arts played in his imagination. In many ways, this is the central crux of his life and work. Inside the catalog are images of nearly every piece from the show, along with extensive commentaries and an endless supply of until now rarely seen photographs, all of which is reproduced in the best of quality. While the rich impasto technique brought about by the substantial gobs of paint plied on by Jess to Duncan's forehead curl of hair in *The Enamored Mage* or Ronald Bladen's swirling abstraction of interior image in *Connie's Painting* is impossible to bring off in a flat two dimension image, novelist Jack Kerouac's doodle of a skeletal figure is clearly visible in Tom Field's aptly titled *Kerouac Painting*. About the only things understandably left out of the catalog are some of the manuscripts and correspondence found in display cases. These are well worth attending to in person, to take note of comments such as Wallace Berman's quip to Duncan after a night stroll outside some strip clubs in Los Angeles: "This city is the lowest & I love it." There's also a substantial display of correspondence, cover art, and art work relating to the poets: Robin Blaser, Robert Creeley, Denise Levertov, Michael McClure, and Charles Olson.

A large, generous amount of work by Jess himself amounts to nearly a quarter of the show. There are several meditations on love and sexuality. One of which is the 1954 gorgeous, tall and narrow *A Thin Veneer of Civility (Self-Portrait)* where a nearly life size Jess in the nude playfully dangles some yarn down to the outstretched paws of a cat turned over onto its back beneath him. The poet W.H. Auden hilariously misread this painting upon seeing it, asking Jess "Why is that man peeing on the cat?" It is a painting perfect for a bathroom interior, full of physical gregarious jovial animalism. A later painting *Lovers III: Erotic Triptych* from 1969 is a richly homoerotic paean to the abiding love found in his relationship with Duncan. These are among the most intimate of paintings by Jess and one of the largest gatherings of them yet held. Small nods to other artists abound, such as the appearance of a miniature-like version of Jay De Feo's *The Rose* in the form of a distant glimmering star over the shoulder of the figure in *Moonset at Sunrise*. There's enough work here to fill a medium-sized room of its own and the full range of his oeuvre is represented.

A number of Jess works commonly referred to as his Paste-ups often get short-changed in favor of larger, more easily viewable pieces. The Paste-ups tend to be smaller, and/or involving what—especially when reproduced in catalogs— appears to be at times near minuscule found text which he's cut up and then arranged in his own manner, successfully queering (both figuratively and oftentimes literally) the original meaning. There has never been a feasible way to reproduce many of them in a published collection without charging an exorbitant price. The publication of *Jess: O! Tricky Cad & Other Jessoterica* (Siglio Press 2012) finally changes that state of affairs. The entire chronological range of Jess' practice within the medium is made available, no more peering into display cases in vain attempting to make out a tiny word or wishing without hope to turn a page over. This volume will never take the place of viewing the original works but it is without doubt an essential tool in future scholarly and leisurely engagement with his work. The intricacy of the Paste-ups world invites reverie. Even the realigned comic shenanigans of *Tricky Cad* and *Nance* where Jess takes his text-collaging practice into the comic strip worlds of Dick Tracy and the Texas Western, not so much transforming them as rather bringing to surface the strangeness lying beneath the casual veneer of the popular everyday mundane found within the world of the strips. Where there are the to-be-expected jokes, they're generally rather muted, avoiding the slapstick. The bits of bizarre dialogue, utter non sequitur, or unusual appearance of say a rather large fish in somebody's lap or hand, strikes the eye as a welcoming invitation to engage with the comic-book world from a newly enhanced perspective.

Among the many nice touches of *Jessoterica* is the fact that the cover-wrappers may be taken off, unfolded, and flipped over to reveal a large 19" by 25" poster of a Jess paste-up. Also Jess' 1960 paste-up chapbook *O!* is included as a separate booklet reprint of the original published by Hawk's Well Press in New York. The chapbook includes a Pre-face written by Duncan in which he sardonically hazards the claim that *O!* is "a book that oughtn't have been done to Art." He continues, offering a fit description and commentary on the Paste-ups as a whole, noting how it is as if Jess offers viewers what's impossibly seen:

> ... a serious alteration in the possibilities, as if one could supply a map given the borderlines of Ernst's *Femme 100 Tetes* and Baum's *Land of Oz*. But Baum was right, the American homeland of the imagination is surrounded by a Deadly Desert and cannot be seen by airplanes. Someplace unseen Jess has built up out of advertizements and old throwaway masterpieces a serial image multi-phasic crowd

With these works Jess relocates common images and
phrases from out the commercially marketed print media
of the everyday world into a visual juxtaposition which
mirrors back a skewed version of reality that is nonetheless
all the more accurate. Immersion into these various scenes
is an oddly familiar experience as if daydreaming away an
afternoon flipping through glossy magazines and the daily
papers. Jess structures his Paste-ups much as daydreams
play off the stored images and information accumulated
within the unconsciousness of the dozing individual. The
images return the regular world to viewers only it is the
world enlarged upon, deepened to such extent, and with
surprisingly perverse magnification, that it astounds with
delightful verisimilitude. Every Paste-up image Jess builds
upon the page is, as Duncan declares *O!*, "an imaginary real
thing for those who look" which endlessly rewards repeated
gazing.

Unlike the relatively broader critical interest and
somewhat positive reception Jess has received over the years,
many of the artists represented in *An Opening of the Field* with
whom he and Duncan mingled have received little or no
critical attention. In a lengthy interview conducted by co-
curator Christopher Wagstaff and published as a pamphlet
(Rose Books 2006), painter Paul Alexander remarks on the
vast discrepancy between concerns shared throughout this
circle of artists with Jess and Duncan at its core, compared
with wider trends occurring within the art world at large:

> ...our work is thought to be either too romantic or too
> pretty or too beautiful in a time when there has been a
> rejection of all that in art. This trend began in the mid-
> sixties which coincided with the middle of my mature
> life, so everything I did and cared about was seen as out

of date and uninteresting to the dealer and the magazine writer. I've almost gotten used to being considered behind the times, though it's been difficult to be told that right to my face by certain people. But I don't feel that it's true about my work at all, and I just want to go on doing it.

This relative disinterest Alexander identifies has been directed on occasion towards not only Jess' work (i.e., "too romantic") but Duncan's as well. Yet over time general broad recognition only continues grow. A similar trend may or may not continue develop in relation to the reception of Alexander's own work, as well as so much other work of the Duncan/Jess household, however this history of past disinterest only makes this show all the more of a surprising revelation and indispensable to any reader of Duncan.

CHAPTER FIVE
ECLIPSED SPEECH: DUNCAN'S LIFE OF LANGUAGE

In 2012 the long awaited biography of San Francisco poet Robert Duncan, *The Ambassador from Venus* by poet Lisa Jarnot finally appeared. Waiting for it as many of its short chapters were published in a broad smattering of periodicals over several years was anticipatory torture. There never seemed a question of *if* it would be published, but *when* was constantly in question. On the other hand, *A Poet's Mind: Collected Interviews* (North Atlantic Books 2012) arrived as a splendid surprise. Unlike with the bio there was little to no anticipatory hub bub surrounding its publication. Which is fairly typical of the most remarkable books, nobody seems to hear about them or be talking them up. The interviews provide rare, unusual, treasured records of Duncan's verbose and challenging imagination; an intimacy which is somewhat lacking in the biography. Both publications join in celebrating the phenomenal rebirth of interest in Duncan's work.

Jarnot guides her readers from Duncan's birth and his subsequent adoption as an infant into a family of Californian theosophists, on to his early discovery of himself both as homosexual and more importantly a poet, to UC Berkeley in the late 1930s, early love affairs, his departure from the West coast, brief marriage (to a woman), early editing and publishing, and his foray into the literary and artistic circles of New York, notably including that of Anais Nin. Jarnot also quiets down some of Duncan's more sensational claims, such as a stint playing the role of a gigolo. She continues tracing the biographical arc of his life back out West and to U.C. Berkeley again in the 1940s, his many friendships, including with poets Jack Spicer and Robin Blaser, his employment at San Francisco State Poetry Center in the 1950s, and his multi-decade work as an advisor on purchases for U.C. Berkeley's Bancroft Library Special Collections. She dutifully records the many lectures and classroom guest appearances he made and provides significant coverage of Duncan's final years of teaching with the nearly cultish milieu gathered about him at the Poetics Program of New College of California in San Francisco's Mission district. Teaching proves to have been an elemental part of Duncan's self-perceived role as poet.

The attention commanded by Duncan's dedication to passing on his personal reading of the poem into the living breath of classroom instruction infected students well beyond the classroom. Poet and critic Peter O'Leary's *Gnostic Contagion: Robert Duncan and the Poetry of Illness* (Wesleyan University Press 2002) chronicles how during Duncan's final years of life as he was teaching in the Poetics Program student poets of the time reported suffering strange effects of ill health all their own. Poets who studied formally as well as informally under Duncan during these years include, among others: Aaron Shurin, Norma Cole, David Lee Strauss, Sarah Menefee, and Susan Thackery. While joining with Duncan in staffing the needs of the Poetics curriculum were Duncan McNaughton, Diane Di Prima, and David Meltzer. As a student in the second manifestation of the program during the late 1990s I sorely regret Jarnot's lack of in depth exploration to this period of time in Duncan's life. Fortunately the oral tales along with photocopies of rare teaching materials and lecture notes are still circulating within the San Francisco poetry community today. Yet a detailed chronological presentation of this history alongside all the rather obscure yet nonetheless available materials is still awaited.

For poets of today faced with the ever growing threat of

environmental catastrophe and the non-stop violence waged around the world in the name of ever-shifting—according to the "elected" political leaders of the day—concepts such as "freedom" and "democracy" Duncan is essential reading. His manifest assertion of the primary, insistent role of the imagination is integral to the future work of any poetry and art which seeks resist pop cultural displays of ironic self-detachment and engage in a sustained resistance to the denigration of a historically grounded recognition of our common humanity. Duncan is a uniquely oracular voice calling for a poetry which moves upon the daily accruement of necessary, practical experience wedded to the extravagant embrace of the fantastical and subversive.

Duncan's interviews provide first hand evidence of the mind which Jarnot tracks the life of. Duncan's perceptions of poetry are by turns demanding, hilarious, inherently anarchic and irreverent. He refused to simplify or overtly explain away matters which often befuddle his readers. He's constantly putting the verbosity extensively commented and documented by Jarnot on full display. Drawing his references and range of subjects from the wide-ranging material which his imagination is constantly revolving around:

> There's an image I'm working on (so I really shouldn't talk about it) having to do with cells and meanings. In cancer, cells are invaded by viruses and the cell is either willing to die, and it then spills out viruses like a pod, or it is unwilling to die and begins to multiply itself instead of multiplying the original virus. Well, metaphorically, *meaning* is like the virus, and the cell can give back those meanings or it can keep the meanings inside and become productive of itself.

The above, for instance, arrives in the context of a discussion with L.S. Dembo regarding the work and influence of Ezra Pound and Charles Olson. Duncan goes on to declare "I proliferate poems all over the place" similar to Olson and Pound, yet doesn't find their poems to be "cancerous." Speaking of his own poems, Duncan contends "they probably are cancerous" but points out "we don't know what the cancer's doing." He then charges onward:

> There are cells which, after all, are individual units and as far as they're concerned the body is just their "neighborhood" or city. Just at a time we're facing overpopulation in our bodies. And in our language we're facing overpopulation. I've got to manage language like someone managing traffic coming in by the twenty tons. I want to see every layer of that traffic.

Continuing on, he easily slips into the slang-riffed comment:

> One of the ways you keep cool with a word is not to remember it's got a life—to let it be just what it was in, say, the eighteenth century. But you don't keep cool if you insist that the story be ever-present. And that's what a cancer is: the cell ever-present; more than one cell in one place.

However, he's quick to point out this isn't a mere flight of fanciful description: "it's not an analogy. It's an activity going on all over the universe and in various areas of ourselves." Duncan concludes by stating his case for believing that:

> human activity is part of the activity of the cosmos [...] life itself, from its beginning cell, is some cooperation of the radioactivity of the sun and the life of the stars and whatever chemicals were present in that first water [...] we are literally—it's no myth—or else it's both myth and reality provided by biophysics—we are so literally children from those rays of the sun and stars...

Dembo is left to make a scrambling recovery "well, all this is very interesting, but it does seem to me that your poetry is often concerned with more specifically human problems, even when it appears to have a cosmic dimension." Readers would be hard put to find a better, more enlightening and entertaining exchange concerning the cosmological poetics of the so-called Black Mountain School.

A complaint I've heard about Jarnot's biography, especially the latter half, is that it reads too much like a smooshed together datebook-transcription-style recounting of Duncan's increasingly frenetic travel/reading itinerary for the many readings, conferences, and visiting professorships. Too often more than anything else we are told where and when he went to read or lecture, who he stayed with, who he dined with, what art shows he looked at, purchases he made, etc. While the travel-log critique is valid, Jarnot also usefully casts a good feeling for the discussions, arguments, and friendships which preoccupied Duncan. While often humorous, such occasions compliment the interviews, attesting to the strength of his commitments. For instance, during the period of his teaching in the Poetics program "Duncan woke in the middle of the night to take half a Valium, preoccupied by a disagreement with Bobbie Louise Hawkins about the scansion of Yeats's 'Second Coming.'" Other somewhat minor details as well, such as an offhand mention by Jarnot of a solo excursion Duncan took between collaborative sessions with the artist R.B. Kitaj while staying abroad in Paris, prove to be chuckle provoking:

> Duncan treated himself to a lighter amusement, taking a trip to a local movie theater to see *Conan the Barbarian*, which had recently opened in Paris in its original English form. Aroused by the hyperdeveloped biceps

46

of its protagonist, Duncan decided that the film was a magnificent anthroposophical-theosophical epic...

Jarnot doesn't quite balance out the travel itineraries with enough of these additional asides, yet there remains plenty enough to avert a glazed over effect coming upon alert readers.

Duncan's 30+ year marriage to the painter Jess and the accompanying household which they set up together is central to his life and work. Jarnot mentions Duncan's early fears of "potential intrusions into their San Francisco household" and in an interview with Gerald Nicosia, Duncan humorously criticizes Beat poets as

> ...people who go streaming into other people's houses and worlds. They were a gang. The difference between a community of poets and the time when you have an adolescence...you have this little brotherhood where everybody shares everything and goes in and out...I didn't even like that in high school...

Duncan was recalling a visit made by Peter Orlovsky, Allen Ginsberg, and Gregory Corso. A visit which Jarnot also references, citing Duncan's description, and accompanying alarm over, from a letter to Denise Levertov:

> Jess who is more seriously alarmed by public-mindedness than I am, and by the assaults of "brotherhood," threw Ginsberg and Peter [Orlovsky] out of the house [...] I do not believe that one can close one's doors to the demand... without a cost of closing one's doors to life: but I am willing to undertake the cost in homage to the household which I worship and draw from.

Jarnot's Chapter 45 "The Household" with its bookcase by bookcase, workspace by workspace, room by room, floor by floor description of 3267 20th Street provides testament to such "homage to the household." Still there's no doubt from Jarnot's account that Duncan had several love affairs as well as deep infatuations over the years and that his frequent traveling served in part to offer the couple possible needed time apart. Now, more than ever, a biography of Jess is well overdue to further round out the full picture of the poet and painter's life together.

Chapter Six
How The Work Works

i. Charting Choral Beginnings: RD's H.D.

> *The image and the tissue of the image, the weaving and the woven tapestry, contain something, the sense of having lived, so that where we respond to books or to works of art intensely we think of them as living, we have the sense of having lived in the world of our reading.*
> Robert Duncan, *The H.D. Book*

In 2011 the first volume of what's proven to be the profoundly historic University of California multiple edition Collected Writings of Robert Duncan made its long awaited appearance in print. Duncan's *H.D. Book* collecting all the chapters of Books 1 and 2 published in various small press journals throughout the 60s, plus extensive notes for a projected Book 3 which Duncan left incomplete. For decades many poets have had their own editions of *The H.D. Book* assembled from various photocopies, or, as was the case for myself, have had access to the PDF of a never realized Frontier Press edition. Nothing, however, compares to reading through the complete book itself in a form as close to possible to one Duncan himself envisioned. Boughn and Coleman edit lightly but with deliberate aim "to arrive at a manuscript as close as possible to the state it was in when Duncan stopped working on it." It is a just service gone long overdue and Duncan's anarchic, cantankerous spirit is no doubt well pleased.

This is one of the ultimate poet's handbooks of personal experience of reading writing. Duncan's concern is wholly himself and he is so completely immersed within it that there is no distracting his personal concerns from the text. This is a lesson to every would-be poet. In your reading as with your writing put your whole self on the line. Giving much needed praise (especially at the time he is writing, 1959-1964) to H.D. is the topic at hand, but there is no way for Duncan not to repeatedly return to his own concerns as he goes along passionately arguing the merit of the older poet's work. Duncan admits, "I am not a literary scholar not a historian, not a psychologist, a professor of comparative religions nor an occultist. I am a student of, I am searching out, a poetics." This list of what he is *not* gives some idea of the array of areas to which he turns his attention and seeks place H.D.'s writing in context, all the while detailing his own habits and approaches to poetry. Duncan busies himself with announcing the poet H.D. never fully becomes while he continually returns to offering instead the poet Robert Duncan is all the while becoming.

During (as well as after) the writing of *The H.D. Book,* Duncan moves into the inarguably mature latter half of his poetic output composing the poems which form his collections from the 1960s: *The Opening of the Field, Roots and Branches,* and *Bending the Bow.* These works chronicle the unfolding of his "Passages" and "Structure of Rime" open-ended poem-sequences which are spread throughout them. For Duncan, the greater, the *truer,* poet is always in a state of becoming, which the "'life' work" of the poems details. He juxtaposes H.D. to Marianne Moore as an example.

> Moore's growth, being periodic, inorganic, has no internal law of the whole. The history of the poem, for Marianne Moore, consists of instances of itself, as natural history

for her is, after Linnaeus and pre-Darwin, a collection of types or models of species. In her technical brilliance (as late as the poem "Style" circa 1956), she excels. The very crux of the poem is its mechanical expertness.

Poetry must move beyond such mere, no matter how exceptional, display of craft. He seeks the union of the poem with the life. Evolution in both the life and the work is everything. He continues the comparison with Moore, aligning H.D.'s "The War Trilogy" which is Duncan's title for what he sees as the key H.D. collections of poems: *The Flowering of the Rod, The Walls Do Not Fall*, and *Tribute to Angels* alongside Ezra Pound's *The Pisan Cantos* and William Carlos Williams' *Paterson*. Moore nowhere approaches what for Duncan is the greater achievement of these works.

> But in her poetics, in her thought and feeling of the poem then, she does not evolve as life does but repeats; her verse is not *creative* but *exemplary* in form. So there is no process of rebirth, of an evolving apprehension of form in her work, of impending experience, that might make for a major impetus in the later years of her life, such as we find in *The Pisan Cantos*, in *Paterson*, and in The War Trilogy, in the work of poets whose poetry had come to be a "life" work.

Throughout *The H.D. Book* continually presents these poets as *the* triumvirate of Modern Poetry in English. Duncan marvels at how content in these epic length long poems is irrevocably interwoven in form and design, the mixing of daily events from past and present being brought into the body of the poem. The result being that "a 'life' appears in the work itself."

To read *The H.D. Book* is to be fully initiated into Duncan's imagination, his world of The Real, where dreams and childhood play inform the poem as vitally as any amount of research or experience in the "adult" world. As he makes clear, "we must discover correspondences and come in reading the poem to read our own lives." Every event, whether imagined or not, must be tested against the imagination. Duncan locates his evidence for the necessity of this among works of philosophy as much as those of poetry and the occult: "'The real world of which the philosophers must take account,' William James writes in his *Principles of Psychology* in 1890, 'is thus composed of the realities plus the fancies and illusions.'" Duncan goes on to declare, "It is 'the total world which *is*' that concerns James; and in his sense that What Is is multifarious" here "James is kin to Emerson before him and to Dewey and Whitehead after." This is likewise true for Duncan with H.D., or for that matter Pound and Williams, D.H. Lawrence or W.B. Yeats as well, poets who owe as much to precursors such as Blake or Dante as to each other. Duncan forms a web extending forward in time as well. Upon the trajectories of which poets such as Norma Cole or Peter O'Leary are to be found. After all, "the quest" which James "projects is not only that of the philosopher who would approach the nature of human experience in its complexity but also that of the poet who seeks a poetics" and it is evident in "the at-homeness in many persons, times and places, that characterizes *The Cantos*, The War Trilogy, and *Paterson*" (again the triumvirate makes its appearance).

This company of fellow poets is of a Whole which is to be sought out and realized in the act of reading. As one's own writing begins emerge, the two activities become at times inseparable, and from such action a greater sense of reality blurs its way into the act of creation. Duncan cites an early influence of such living writing in the figure of St. Francis of Assisi, a version he picks up from the historian Ernst Kantorowicz who "sees Francis as a poet, for he lived in this world, it seems to the historian as if it were in the eternal presence of all things; he lived in metaphor as if it were not a mere device of rhetoric but were a reality of what was." So Duncan would have us all do—yet he is also quick to discourage the poetry of mere "self-expression." The poem under hand is not to be made available to serve pedestrian needs. For "the poet takes over as a higher person from the immediate social personality" and "the work of art appears as a gift for another but also as a means for another to be there. Self-expression may be an urgency of art, but the self has no expression except in this other" Duncan believes "self-expression and likewise self-possession in verse would set up an 'I' that is the private property of the writer in the place of the 'I' in which all men may participate." This is an invaluable guiding principle that is made clear in H.D.'s work which "like Dante, like John of Patmos, has no experience that is not meaning, that is not, by emblem or rubric, part of feeling beyond her feeling. The events of her life are not only personal, they are also hints of a great universe to which all man's fictions belong."

Duncan demonstrates how "the word verse" is rooted in the action of the plough preparing the field for harvest:

As men plough forward and back, did they once write, turning
?enil eht fo dne eht ta

And he does not fail to take note that "It is a fanciful etymology" His delight in poetry is rooted in such stuff. It is among the many pleasures found in *The H.D. Book*, the act of which writing he tells us he undertook, "for I needed this book for a place for her to exist in me." During the time span of Duncan's own generation H.D. was met with vehemence by poetry book reviewers such as Randall Jarrell, poet-men who "live uneasily with or under the threat of genius women" and in whose reviews it is not clear "what H.D.'s work is, but it is most clear, if we accept unquestioningly all that comes from his authority, that whatever it is it is 'silly,' 'level debris,' 'anachronism'—not to be countenanced by reasonable men." And it was in such a negative, limited poetry world Duncan sought to establish and declare his own poetic reasoning. A fertile assemblage of various texts all braced up by one another bound by such abiding principles as "the poem comes as a gift to the poet writing." His fastidious faith to poetry as an order above and beyond all others was monumental and rock solid with H.D. as a founding force.

ii. Writing Reading Writing: Duncan's "Mirrord" Poetics

With publication of Duncan's *The Collected Later Poems and Plays* and *The Collected Essays and Other Prose* the heyday of Duncan publication reached its zenith. Finally everything Duncan published is readily available to readers, or rather nearly everything. There's still a few dozen uncollected pieces of prose listed in an appendix in back of *Collected Essays* which await publication in a future volume, perhaps alongside transcriptions of lectures and/or interviews likewise left out of the ever terrific *A Poet's Mind: Collected Interviews* (North Atlantic).

Throughout his working life, Duncan proved himself nothing if not verbose. As exhaustive a talker as he was prolific a writer, he evolved a practice of always being in process of developing ideas while in the very act of explicating upon them. One result of his colossal output is that much of the as-of-now uncollected material likely duplicates statements readily found in *Collected Essays and Other Prose*.

The Collected Later Poetry and Plays represents the assured completion of the vital gathering underway with *The Collected Early Poetry and Plays*. These two volumes confirm that the canon of Duncan's poetry is fully established and readily available to a broad audience. Each collection gathered and published by Duncan is reproduced with sections of uncollected individual poems grouped by year published appearing in between and substantial notes in back give further details concerning much of the work.

There is more than a hint of unorthodox, wide open yet nonetheless priestly sacrament to these texts. We're undoubtedly at the brink of a too long in coming renaissance of fevered interest in and appreciation for Duncan's substantial contribution to Poetic Orders.

The Opening of the Field (1960) fittingly opens *The Collected Later Poems and Plays* as therein Duncan achieves mastery of his mature poetic powers with complete clarity. The initial poem "Often Am I Permitted to Return to a Meadow" has been so heavily anthologized, as well as rather regrettably lampooned, it remains perhaps Duncan's most recognized poem. *Opening of the Field* is also where the first of his open-ended poem sequences "Structures of Rime" finds its beginnings.

Two poetry collections later, in *Bending the Bow* (1968), the initial entries of the second sequence "Passages" begin appear. These two sequences continue with over-lapping regularity throughout the later work. In the final decades of his life, Duncan enters into his canonical self-defining practice of poetics structured upon a seamless weaving of the dual activity *writing reading / reading writing* in a vast web of textual congress.

Duncan finds within this activity of, as he writes it, "writing/reading or reading/writing" it is

...not myself, or *the* Self, but yet another dimension, the
work Itself, the poem Itself, where Poetry Itself appeard.
The poem, not the poet, seeks to be immortal and must go
deep enough into its mortality to come to that edge.
("The Self in Postmodern Poetry")

All of Duncan's late work hinges upon ever greater
actualization of this "edge" where one's actions are never
found to be easily definable byway of type, method, or
otherwise familiarly known modules typically sought after
for defining the activity at hand. "To read" then comes to
be seen as being at the business of "writing" as much as "to
write" then is set within the experience of "reading"; the
mirrored, or as in Duncan's more often favored spelling style
for both poems and prose "mirrord", activities spurring each
other on.

Reading Duncan's prose alongside his poems, this practice
becomes ever the more evident as a central feature of his
formal development. Not only does Duncan endlessly bring
his prose and poetry together alongside one another—several
texts appear duplicated by both volumes, there being at times
no clear cut separation for editors to abide by—he constantly
seizes opportunity of testifying to his own experience of how
fluidly and often writing / reading merge to one vast pulsing
draw of energy.

He locates another identity in the activity that is the
Poem or Poetry itself, whether he's writing his own work
or reading that of Walt Whitman or William Shakespeare
(two poets who like Dante and William Blake, or Duncan's
contemporaries such as Charles Olson and Robert Creeley, or
Jack Spicer and Robin Blaser, Duncan repeatedly references
as integral to his own work).

...an incarnation of that Presence of a Poetry. This body
of words the medium of this spirit. Writing or reading,
where words pass into this commanding music, I found a
presence of person more commandingly real than what I
thought to be my person before; Whitman or Shakespeare
presenting more of what I was than I was. And in the
course of my own poetry what has drawn me into its
depths is this experience of a more intense presence of
world and self than I know in myself.
("Changing Perspectives in Reading Whitman")

The personal tone adopted here is found ever increasingly
in Duncan's later work, throughout the 1970s into the 1980s
until his death in 1988, as his aging body notably enters into
his writing. One striking occurrence is evidenced by the
poem "Let Me Join You Again This Morning, Walt Whitman"
one of the texts present in both collections.

Duncan included the poem at the end of his talk/essay
"The Adventure of Whitman's Line" originally published
in the inaugural issue of the short-lived New College of
California Poetics journal *Convivio*, in which context the
poem finds inclusion in *Collected Essays*, while also having
never been gathered by Duncan into a collection of his poetry
it appears in the *Collected Later Poems* within "Uncollected
Work: 1969-1982."

[...]

telling too the way the limbs move from an aging spine, courage now in this
persisting, the pains-telling a new phase of the life-story, you at thirty-seven,
Whitman, setting out,

I now at sixty read again, remembering—but you too inhabiting all ages remembered
in the rejoicing memorial of man's identity in each step you take—my own
being at thirty-seven

in the opening of the field of grass you made for me facing the nation we inhabit together
aged in the wood Dante in the darkly bewildered *selva oscura* set out from
and returns to—the human condition—almost with despair but persisting

Duncan situates his physical health in relation to Whitman's boisterous call for a Nationalist Poetics (which many, including Duncan, have also identified as Imperialistic) yet his concern always remains focused on the poem-at-hand and its relation to poetry-at-large, ever integral to both his own person as well as a larger sense of humanity in which any one of us participates.

The physical condition of Duncan's health, for better or worse, is of no concern other than it is the actual state in which he thus finds himself as he writes, as he reads, but in Whitman finds relinquishment to an ever encouraging, greater order.

Alternately, another example may be seen in the late poem "To Master Baudelaire" from Duncan's final collection *Ground Work II: In the Dark* (1987) where Duncan, experiencing "The Baudelairean words" launches into a reverie full of deep resonance with Baudelaire's envisioning of experience, what Duncan terms "His Malaise":

> ...this world,

> this great moving image, just now beginning again to be
> troubled, yet, as if Eternity had a hold there, at last,
> lasting, and I in that hold held,   I, held here, to the last,
> in your searching yourself in me,   in my reflecting.

Duncan encourages his readers to see this activity of "writing / reading" which proves central to his creative life as likewise central to their own. Welcoming into their "reading / writing" lives this figure of Poetry. Again and again, Duncan promulgates the practice. He's relentlessly sounding the depths of his experience of it, probing its workings and sharing his discoveries where he finds them. As in his Afterword for Beverly Dahlen's *The Egyptian Poems*:

What is the nature of this voice in poetry? It is compelling. It comes from "below"— a speech below speech; it comes from behind speech. Not from an unconscious below and behind consciousness, for this is a consciousness below and behind consciousness: that is its force. The "I" itself has undergone a change from the personal "I." Where "I" is an other, as Rimbaud saw. The psychic life she draws in writing may be drawn from her own psychic life, but here its body is the text and it speaks to the psyche of the reader as reader. For the readers too, "I" is an other, as he or she takes identity in the text.

There is no doubting the sincerity of Duncan's insistent calling for such recognition from his readers. He isn't kidding around. Poetry spoke to him and he recognized within it a power to affect profound recognition.

> In the vocation of Poetry, some poetry yet to be calls us, "wounds" invisibly, or appoints us, and the "I" passes beyond this "we" (in which the intent to write becomes lost in the conflagration of readings) into a void of person where it is the absence of the Book that needs not the writer but the writing in order to present itself.
> ("The Delirium of Meaning")

This is not a practice meant for private isolation either. It is public business, utterly inclusive. Not just literature for study in the university but art meaningful to needs of broader society.

> Whitman's politics, like Dante's, is the politics of a polis that is a poem. In both the Preface of 1855 and *Democratic Vistas* Whitman insists that the heart or soul of this matter of America and of democracy is poetic. He comes not to bring a new religion but to bring—more faithful to the truth of things than religion—a poetry.
> ("Changing Perspectives in Reading Whitman")

For Duncan the poet is always attending to the revelation of the poem in the world around him.

> As I write, the writing talks to me. In the Orphic tradition, poets could understand the language of birds and trees. Listening to the roar of the waves, voices appear. It is only a story we are making up, but it comes *to* us. We find we are living, suffering, loving, dying a story. We had not known otherwise.
> ("Man's Fulfillment in Order and Strife")

Duncan feels enabled by the activation of this "story" working its way on its own behalf to find the means via his role as the poet-host whereby to realize its occurrence. Allowing the poem to lead the way, he relinquishes his interest in exerting overt control over where it may lead. Instead he gives over both his effort and interest to the achieving of unknown ends, as his work progresses he is more than ever listening rather than directing.

> I started a series without end called "Structures of Rime" in which the poem could talk to me, a poetic seance, and, invoked so, persons of the poem appeared as I wrote to speak. I had only to keep the music of the invocation going and to take down what actually came to me happening in the course of the poem. Lawrence tells us that, once he was at work on a novel his characters took over, having their own life there. [...] the poet searches out the actuality of the world into which he extends what is now *his* world of Self—his search transformed into an art—in order to realize in imagination the world. From the reality of this order, an "interior" feeling that has its heart in the apprehension of universe, being and even self, more real than he is, speak to him.
> ("Man's Fulfillment in Order and Strife")

This unveiling of the process of the poem "to realize in imagination the world" within the poem itself as it enters into being is ushered in by how one lives; the literal surroundings within which daily life occurs. An aspect Duncan readily acknowledges having learned from visual artists, particularly his partner Jess and other artists, such as Harry Jacobus, moving within their close social circles tied together by friendship and art.

> ...I see both Jess and Harry Jacobus in their work as relating in turn to my own development as a poet—-for they have brought the imagination into painting again, as I have worked to bring the imagination into poetry. They work with a consciousness of metaphor and symbol, of color and form as terms of a magic.
> ("Statement on Jacobus for Borregaard's Museum")

The household plays a central role for Duncan as the generative, nurturing cauldron site of the imagination.

> ...we see that the rooms we live in are haunted by our living; that we live in ashes of lavender, in blue lights, in burning orange or luminous gold of ourselves.
> ("Statement on Jacobus for Borregaard's Museum")

The textual ground Duncan urges the poem move on is the actual sounding it evokes: "In the realized poem, the poem that is *sound* thruout, the poet attends even as we do the order of what the poem is saying." ("From Notes on the Structure of Rime") Again, the poet's body serves as conduit for forces exerted by demands of the poem.

> The heart, the brain, the nervous system—that tree of immediate, intricately branching, correlations thruout the body— the visceral, deep inward, tonal condition, are united in one governance in that passion from which all the projected field of "content" and "affect," of "message" and of "invention," arises as the living body or *form*, the very *poem* of that always particular, always urgent, always

unique demand that a poetry come into existence.
("From Notes on the Structure of Rime")

Early on in his own vocation as a poet, Duncan locates the roots of his conceiving how the poem moves in Ezra Pound's achievements with free verse:

> He found an imperative in poetry when one "must" write in free verse, "when the 'thing' builds up a rhythm more beautiful than that of set metres, or more real, more a part of the emotion of the 'thing,' more germane, intimate, interpretative than the measure of regular accentuated verse." Craft here is not to impose a form upon a force but to find the force, the very movement of shape, sound and meaning, in which the form of the total process is apprehended.
> ('The Lasting Contribution of Ezra Pound')

Following his Poet-Masters, such as Pound, releases Duncan from any struggle with originality, in fact he delights in being derivative. He enjoys echoing the works he loves wherefrom he finds his own powers as Poet to be drawn.

Duncan's poem "After Shakespeare's Sonnet 76" announces itself as being drafted in the "casual imprint that is the Bolinas style" (referencing the small coastal community of Bolinas, CA a sometime manic haven for poets during the early 1970s). In the notes for this uncollected poem, which appeared in an issue of Bolinas resident poet Duncan McNaughton's *Fathar*, is Duncan's description of it in a notebook as written in "the modern anti-genteel mode / of the post-Poundian era / 1920-1970."

His "Second Take on Sonnet 76" published with the first in the same issue of *Fathar*, returns with seriousness to what proves an ever common theme for Duncan: joining in with a larger company, vaster than imaginable, that is never graspable by a single poem or poet alone, but is an ongoing roar of voices adding to a common response. That "writing / reading" pageantry which festoons all poetry within a never ending tale of old:

> ...I rage,
> O Love, as deep as others rage, the din,
> the news, drowns out the music. Still the old
> way Love pursues in which our tale was ever told.

Duncan leaves us with the feeling the Poem will always be of necessary demand; composed for and by a great eternal community of the like-minded; who although separated across centuries and continents apart, are yet driven outside any rational comprehension to join each other in rising song.

Chapter Seven
"Liberation In Time Of Emergency"
Strange-?-Pairings:
Duncan & Frank O'hara

*Whitman calls for an end of the Old World gods, the thralldom
of ancient bonds to the codes of what the Lord abominates or
the relentless Goddess demands, and Frank O'Hara, in this a
true fellow to Whitman, in my own time calld again for such
a Liberation in Time of Emergency.*

Robert Duncan

In the passage quoted as epigraph above from the intended
Preface to his late collection *Ground Work: Before the War* (New
Directions 1984), Robert Duncan recognizes Frank O'Hara's
work as an essential resource in time of need, holding it up
as essential mythic poet lore in line with Whitman as well
as "Old World gods" (a lineage in which Duncan viewed
his own work as being aligned). In closing this book-length
essay into Duncan's prodigious life work in poetry, I offer this
reading of essay collections on each of the two, Duncan and
O'Hara, in hopes of widening the parameters of a reading of
American poetry which classifies poets into distinct schools
or group byway of style or geographical location. More than
ever such lines of reading are arbitrary demarcations serving
little to no purpose, failing to recognize that our reading
writing / writing reading lives are in fact the Grand Collage
Duncan's work attests and calls for in response.

Most welcome and necessary are these collections of new
essays *Re:)Working the Ground: Essays on the Late Writings of
Robert Duncan* edited by James Maynard (Palgrave Macmillan
2012) and *Frank O'Hara Now: New Essays on the New York Poet*

edited by Robert Hampson and Will Montgomery (Liverpool University Press 2011). Poets of literary imagination of the first rank, Duncan and O'Hara each contributed divergent but complimentary perspectives to American poetry of the latter half of the twentieth century. Ezra Pound is daddy to them as much as Gertrude Stein is momma. Play, mirth, and wit with plenty of informal as well as formal reading and study informs the grid-work anchoring the poems and life of these poets. They live according to the life of the poem that is in them, firmly refusing to have any sense of their art as separate from the rest of their daily affairs. In this, these two serve as models beyond compare.

Both Duncan and O'Hara share in common an open homosexuality, at odds with society of their time, that is central to their identity, along with a predilection for surrounding themselves with visual artists—O'Hara wrote art criticism, worked at MOMA, modeled for painter friends, the likes of Larry Rivers to Grace Hartigan— Duncan settled into setting up a household with his life-partner the artist Jess in San Francisco which lasted until Duncan's passing in 1988 and during which time together they befriended several San Francisco artists from Wallace Berman's *Semina* group to the filmmaker Stan Brahkage who lived with them for a time in his youth. Each is politically committed in his own fashion, within the poetry world (the infamous feuds between Duncan/Jess and Jack Spicer, later his defense of Zukofsky against Barrett Watten; O'Hara's social-poetic juxtaposition reading "Poem 'Lana Turner has collapsed'" whilst sharing the stage with Robert Lowell) as well as the public domain, taking firm stances against the oppressive gloom of the 1950s racial and sexual mores (Duncan's groundbreaking essay "The Homosexual in Society," O'Hara's strident interracial friendship with LeRoi Jones/Amiri Baraka).

Yet each poet remains distinguishable from the other; most notably by way of how personality manifests itself in the work, a matter of style and taste. O'Hara is very much the singular poet of Manhattan and all the protoplasmic buzz of activity that's to be found there, while San Francisco with that ever vibrant West Coast ethos is indelibly tied to Duncan's poetic mythos. For O'Hara's poems are fast, full of witty remarks, quick-moving and in the world in which he is living. Current events are abundant, both personal and public. Whereas Duncan's poems are shrouded in a projection of his own life's reading, deeply otherworldly while ever-pursuing profoundly mystical insight. Events occurring within the poems are timeless as he weaves references from ancient lore on up through the entire Western tradition of thought into a seamless blanketed cape of his own uniquely startling vision. The discussion of the poetry behind these charismatic figures will be long lasting and unlikely exhaustible any time soon.

While the great wealth of critical material readily available on O'Hara is continually expanding, rarely does the writing measure up to what's on hand in this collection superbly gathered by Robert Hampson and Will Montgomery. All the essays are exemplarily readable and nearly as entertaining reading as O'Hara's work itself, making the book tremendously rewarding and quite the surprise. Hampson and Montgomery note that "the O'Hara that is quite so widely known and loved is often not quite the same O'Hara that we, in our separate ways, have loved." They set out looking "to suggest that O'Hara is not as easily assimilable — or indeed as friendly — as he might appear." There should be no doubt that they do indeed succeed in achieving this goal. As they point out, O'Hara's "poems can be difficult and recalcitrant, their surface fluency concealing obdurate lacunae and hesitation. O'Hara's cheerfulness is the cheerfulness of one who has encountered and embraced suffering. The ready wit conceals doubt and uncertainties." And one essential component of their success in presenting a fresher, broader view of the poet is contained in their "desire to produce a response to O'Hara that had a transatlantic dimension" so when seeking contributions they drew "in established and emerging voices from both sides of the Atlantic" resisting any easy slide into formulaic flack.

For each subsequent generation of poets O'Hara's work consistently proves an energizing force, fertile ground over and over again for sparking lively poems derived from out reading his own, the best of which resist being wholly imitative. O'Hara is often cast as "Frank" in such work as if he's readily around, a pal these poets might be meeting for a commiserating drink during a rough patch, personal and poetic. Reading these essays leaves the feeling that the writer approaches writing on O'Hara as if the essay-form might allow itself to be a poem. I'm not saying these essays are in any way hybrid or otherwise experimental in form, but the over-all charge that is felt, the vibe as leaps in connections are made and the abundant quotes of O'Hara and others in relation to him pour forth, unleashes a steady thrill that long outlasts first reading.

David Herd's "Stepping out with O'Hara" centers round the demonstration "that in O'Hara's poetry he allows his thought to settle around the gesture of the step." Much as mentioned above, his poems are occasions full of such charge that the reader feels as if we're out for a stroll with the poet himself. As Herd says "one quite readily finds oneself thinking about the way he places his feet" and "one thinks about it because he [O'Hara] thinks about it." O'Hara's projected presence is so near viscerally manifest within his poems. It is not surprising that when speaking of O'Hara's 'Poem [light clarity avocado salad in the morning]' Josh Robison offers up a reading of "O'Hara's Poetics of Breath" wagering that in an O'Hara poem "breath is presented as essential to cognition, which is itself something almost immediate, a bodily state of being" and "the speaker presents an intense degree of familiarity not with the absent addressee but rather with his own body: 'and all thoughts disappear in a strange quiet excitement/ I am sure of nothing but this, intensified by breathing'." Adding to Herd's comments on O'Hara's "step," Rod Mengham notes how "In O'Hara, the poet-as-walker and his reveries are equally mobile. In fact, the later poet maintains an equilibrium between the claims of the virtual and the real."

O'Hara enjoyed having a body and celebrating in its occupation of space. The preponderance of instances of his likeness being conveyed in artworks by friends and associates, and which he no doubt took much pleasure in, mirrors the prevalent physicality of presence within his writing. As Redell Olsen's essay focusing on O'Hara and the painter Grace Hartigan reminds us "O'Hara is similarly noted for his collaborative self-staging through both photography and art. The artists Jane Freilicher, Nell Blane, Larry Rivers, Grace Hartigan, Phillip Guston, Alex Katz, and Fairfield Porter all painted portraits of O'Hara." Reading O'Hara's poems the references to his body are inescapable, as are those to artist friends who convey its image in numerous works of art. There's no commentary possible which refuses acknowledge the actions of O'Hara's busy social life amongst artists. As John Wilkinson comments on how in "O'Hara's *Odes* works of art are presented and become present as at once marmoreal and pulsing, exact, mobile and sexual — and this is true of the *Odes* themselves." He continues arguing that the *Odes* "work within a Romantic project, and a secular one:

the confusion of unborn, living, dead and undead, and the unbinding of tenses." Wilkinson sees the odes demonstrative of O'Hara's poems as physical manifestations that exist in the instant: "The artwork lives and dies only in encounter."

Undeniably it is in the encounter that O'Hara thrives. A humming electiveness that in Nick Selby's consideration of memorial artworks to O'Hara by Jasper Johns and Joe Brainard shows itself in:

> the pressure of such a reimagining of the poet's body that we have seen in relation to the work of Joe Brainard and Jasper Johns that is, I want to argue, absolutely critical to the power and affectivity of 'In Memory of my Feelings'. By continually renegotiating its relationship to the poet's actual body this is a poem that courts ambiguity, and juxtaposition, in order to discover the poetic possibilities of living as variously as possible. The closing lines of the poem resonate powerfully because of their ability to demonstrate *feelingly* how O'Hara's sense of being in the poem is subject to his exploration of a complex set of relationships between performative positions available to him as poet. While sounding sincere, authentically troubled by the sense of lost feelings and the poetic occasion that calls for their memorializing, the poem's closing moments also announce that its nostalgia for a lost self is a mere performance, a ruse in which intimacy and feeling-ness, even the body itself, are exposed as effects of the poet's textual negotiations:

> and I have lost what is and always and everywhere present, the scene of my selves, the occasion of these ruses, which I myself and singly must now kill
> and save the serpent in their midst.

Daniel Kane's extensive commentary on O'Hara's collaboration with film artist Alfred Leslie on *The Last Clean Shirt* probes similar territory, as O'Hara mined lines from "In memory of my Feelings" for the subtitles he provides for the film where "film becomes poetry — or film interacts with poetry. Or poetry extends film." As Kane describes: "such moves invite the spectator/reader experiencing the no-longer-autonomous work of art to 'pay attention', to participate in making meaning in response to a form that no longer adheres to conventional definitions of genre." It is such challenging and subversive tendencies which draw in readers ensuring there will always be an audience for O'Hara's work. He sticks you full throttle behind the moving set-changes of the poem, revealing and concealing as the surprises keep arriving. There's nothing quite like it.

The fast moving flexibility in the best of these essays responds in kind to this energy embodied by O'Hara's poems; working through the poems with the same quickness of combining careful logic with fast action, risking absurdity, perhaps, but nonetheless making connections not matched—at least in energy—by previous critics. Will Montgomery's tackling of the comparison and relationship of O'Hara's verse to that of avant-garde composer Morton Feldman provides example:

> Although O'Hara rejects an all-encompassing 'poetics', I think it is possible to identify an important attraction to instability in his thinking in his praise of a quasi-metaphysical 'unpredictability' in Feldman. Feldman sought to let 'sounds exist in themselves — not as symbols, or memories which were memories of other music to begin with'. His aim in this early work to 'unfix' the formal relationships between 'rhythm, pitch, dynamics' is broadly comparable to O'Hara's rejection of a 'poetics' of 'form, measure, sound, yardage, placement, and ear'. Feldman too scorns metre, seeking to recover a more complex and subjective experience of temporality: 'I am not a clockmaker. I am interested in getting to time in its jungle — not in the zoo.' In this last statement, Feldman is close, I think, to the formal and conceptual negations

of some of O'Hara's poems — the nihilism of 'Hatred', for example, the darkness that fringes some of the Odes, or the dizzying temporal and referential leaps of 'Second Avenue' or 'Biotherm'.

It is high time for such fabulous reading of terrific work. *Frank O'Hara Now* serves its purpose and then some. These essays bring acuity combined with a strong dose of good cheer. There's a new standard set here, not only in future critical assessment of O'Hara, but that of his contemporaries as well.

After what felt a notable lapse in critical attention from academics as well as publishers, Duncan's work has been garnering further well-deserved notice. The multi-volume *Collected Writings* only further that this is the time for celebrating the worthy contribution Duncan's work will undoubtedly continue offer. An ongoing cause that *(Re:) Working The Ground* is in part the product of, as editor James Maynard notes: "This book began as a series of papers presented at a three-day symposium entitled '(Re:)Working the Ground: A Conference on the Late Writings of Robert Duncan,' which took place in the Poetry Collection at the University at Buffalo April 20-22, 2006. This event celebrated the republication by New Directions of *Ground Work: Before the War/In the Dark*" Duncan's final two collections of poems published together in a single volume. Stephen Fredman reminds us how Duncan himself established the significance of the original 1983 publication of the first of these final volumes of his poems, writing in 1972 "I do not intend to issue another collection of my work since *Bending the Bow* until 1983 at which time fifteen years will have passed."

Although subtitled "essays on the late writings of Robert Duncan" and while the focus throughout is on the poetry found in *Groundwork*, the majority of contributions take advantage of the quite circular nature of Duncan's poetic practice in order to revisit earlier writings while in the process addressing the later work. The result is that unfamiliar readers are not left behind in the larger discussion. These explorative essays into Duncan's oeuvre serve to provoke initial readings of the poems and entice a fresh generation of scholars as well as poets into their own explorations of the wonders spun in Duncan's arcana. This is especially the case since *Groundwork* is not so much a life's summation of poetic work, as *The H.D. Book* is a mid-life's summation of reading, but rather a realization of the work's own being. In these later poems, Duncan is as if afloat among texts whose language comes to life adrift around him as he samples as he may. These essays assist with gaining a firm foothold amidst the swirling wonder that is Duncan's work.

As noted above this collection brings to print a previously unpublished Preface which at one point was intended for the original publication of *Before the War*. Drafted in a notebook by Duncan and left off incomplete, for those readers dedicated to as complete an understanding as possible of the weave Duncan throws across his writing, this is the literal cat's meow. Reminiscent of Duncan's reading diary style he implements in *The H.D. Book,* as well as previous prefaces to his earlier volumes, even left incomplete, there's plenty here offering fresh introspection into Duncan's practice. Also printed here is a short poem, "In Passage," which was originally intended as preface for *In the Dark*. The closing line demonstrates the subtle powers shaping the exchanges between Duncan's reading and writing, where he situates a statement of prime intent he holds to in all his work: "what I divine I come into and change."

Maynard's telling of the source for Duncan's inspiration for the title *In the Dark* gives example of Duncan's tendency to "divine" and thereby have rights to "change," making his own claim to use whatever material serves his purposes:

> ...despite its many suggestive associations with alchemy, Norman Austin's book *Archery at the Dark of the Moon* (1975), James Hillman's *The Dream and the Underworld* (1979), and its appearance in several different contexts throughout these same notebooks—the phrase "in the dark" officially announced itself to Duncan from one of his favorite pulp genres: science fiction. In this case, it was the opening chapter of Andre Norton's novel *Forerunner Foray* (1973), with its description of the protagonist Ziantha's membership in an intergalactic organization of psychically gifted thieves: "She was part of an organization that operated across the galaxy in a loose confederacy of shadows and underworlds. Governments might rise and fall, but the Guild remained, sometimes powerful enough to juggle the governments themselves, sometimes driven undercover to build in the dark." Compare this passage to one of Duncan's earlier descriptions of *Ground Work*: "*Underground Work*, the 'new book' might be called: not the 'underground' of the Revolution, but the underground of a life not in tune with the powers that rule above."

In full confirmation of this being Duncan's source, Maynard relates in a footnote, "this exact quotation, dated March 25, [1982], appears in Notebook 66 with the note: 'In the opening chapter of Andre Norton's *Forerunner Foray* I think I have found the title of Ground Work II: 'in the dark.'" For Duncan the separation of literature into distinction of genres, some considered more literary than others, bares little merit when it comes to what's fuel for furthering his own writings. He pulls from all over as needed, and as come upon. At times, as seen above, readings of a later date might lead to alteration and expansion upon an earlier idea or thought in writing. Nothing for Duncan is textually static, but rather fluid, and thus in eternal transformation as the interactions of reading and writing continually feed off each other, propelling the comprehensively combined action of which *Groundwork* is accumulative example.

As Eric Keenagham picks up on, "For Duncan, poetic composition is first and foremost an act of *reading,* which itself is the cornerstone of secular humanism." A few pages further on continuing:

> Ultimately, we are *readers.* Our own reading praxes can be read in light of how Duncan himself would characterize that activity as an engaged participation in the process of life itself—rather than a removed position of Kantian judgment—and how he characterized reading as the means for bringing his own agency as a writer and a humanist into a productively aporetic crisis. It even produces a new kind of political engagement.

Or as Robert J. Bertholf summarizes a passage from Duncan's poem-series "The Regulators": "The appeal is for the Muse to enter history and change the nature of our lives by altering what government regulates so that the message of the song will be present and available 'where we wonder.'" Duncan expects others to continue the practice his own project takes up. At least in part, Duncan seeks to breed responsibility into his readers. There's an urgency to respond in kind that's welcomed and called for by the work. Duncan intends his poetry to participate ad infinitum as part of an ongoing conversation to engage with and alter the world's imagination.

This aspect of Duncan's poetics is expanded on by Devin Johnston in his discussion "Poems from the Margins of Thom Gunn's 'Moly'" (these poems were written by Duncan during his unanticipated immersion in an interactive reading of Thom Gunn's "Moly," while on a bus trip on a reading tour): "In terms of compositional practice, Duncan did not make firm distinctions between marginalia, inspiration, and translation: for him, all three constitute responsive or reactive dimensions of poetry. By habit and conviction, he thought that writing should arise spontaneously from reading, blurring the line between the two activities." In his closing Johnston emphasizes: "for Duncan as for Gunn, poetry proposes no settled relations or certain origins but remains essentially reactive or responsive. It might include translation from one language to another or a mysterious transference of love from one person to another, according to the rhymes and resemblances that run throughout Duncan's writing."

The looping nature of Duncan's poems, due to his tendency to reach out and draw from texts he's reading as he's writing in order to service the needs of the writing, leads to his referring to himself as "a derivative poet." Stephen Collis argues this self-identification of Duncan's is evidence of his worry over "poetry's 'real estate.'" Collis suggests we "see in Duncan's use of the term a concern for the status of poetry as *property*. Indeed, I suggest that this was very much his increasing concern during the 1970s and his 'slow down' in production between 1968 and 1984. Duncan, in this reading, is revealed to be a critic of intellectual property and a defender of *the poetic commons*." Collis distinguishes between "Duncan's most extreme expressions of derivation and literary 'commoning'—his 'emulations, imitations, reconstruals,' et cetera of the metaphysical poets and Dante" alongside the "outright appropriation of found materials" claiming that "Duncan's 'duplications' operate within a quasi-academic 'citational economy,' with the poet, in most instances, *acknowledging* his sources." In his own work, both critical and creative, Collis pursues the use of just such means to reach tremendously useful results for encouraging an activist-minded engaged poetics of which Duncan would no doubt approve.

There's a new wealth of interest in writing on Duncan by poet-scholars such as Collis, following in the wake of figures such as Nathaniel Mackey and Lisa Jarnot. This work continues yield a bevy of potential readings for a future which proves Duncan's weighty presence shall likely endure. Duncan's hands, as it were, are alive in the vivid influence he plays in the creative works by such critics. Peter O'Leary's unpacking of the appropriation of angelology in "Duncan's Celestial Hierarchy," rightly gives fair warning that "Duncan's approach to these angelic powers is predatory—but the "gnostic" invasion he imagines stains his later work not as a form of knowledge but as one of disease;" as O'Leary points out, "the pleasure of these poems doesn't come from *solving* them or *answering* them but from reading them." Readers infected as O'Leary by Duncan's "disease" suffer in delight. As Duncan writes in the poem intended but not included as preface of *In the Dark*, "in time you must terrify." This directive is to the poem, the poet, as well as the reader of the poem; all three after all are in some sense the same. Accepting Duncan's terms on the level he literally did himself, i.e. life or death, no joke; it should come as no surprise if we do "terrify" ourselves on occasion. These are times without solace.

Duncan's work demands of readers, as it should, as total an embrace as he himself gives, his willingness to release hold when writing, no clinging "to the self", is reflected in Brian M. Reed's study of correlations between Duncan's work and that of Gertrude Stein. Duncan, "like Stein in the late 1920s, more narrowly inquires into the act of composition and corollary problems of identity and representation. He works from the premise that 'ideas' and 'the self' are not independent entities that an author can mirror in a poem. Instead, they come into being in the very process of 'writing writing'." Writing is never an activity Duncan takes lightly. He seeks a universal depth transcending present realities in his role of poet-as-assembler. Working on the poems in *Groundwork* his sense of purpose only intensifies. As Clément Oudart quotes from a letter Duncan writes to his friend, Australian poet Chris Edwards:

> With a note of urgency in his remark, Duncan pointed out that besides an essential 'kindred strain...the art needs too the foundational—to address the 'ground'—and the declaration and carrying through of an architecture.' Duncan's constant grappling with the origin of creation (*poiesis*)—his perpetual attempt to find, found, and sound the ground(s) of his restless poetic practice—is embedded in his (at times abyssal) grounding in intertextuality.

Readers should not to be turned off by Duncan's frequent realignment of sources but rather recognize the openly inviting greeting in his wanton collaging of texts that is his intention.

Dennis Tedlock relates hearing from Robert Bertholf how "when [Duncan] took a notebook with him somewhere, he often left it behind, which is why he was careful to write 'Return to Robert Duncan' and his street address on the first page of each notebook." A trick to up the ante on the writing the notebook contains or a sign of willingness to have the writing be freed of ownership? I myself know poet friends who would be inclined to use such a trick to compel a soft edginess into their current manuscripts; intentionally introducing the threat that their handwritten drafts of poems might be found in the hands of indiscriminate strangers. A threat which while perhaps minor is nonetheless real all the same: even imaginary, such threat might swell a manuscript with force that would otherwise be absent. While impossible to fully ascertain Duncan's intention behind the practice it is clear he relished the freedom provided by so relinquishing his personal ownership of writing.

For Duncan, as with O'Hara, poems are fleeting and ethereal *yet sustained as acts*; grounded byways where the dedication of the poet's life to the writing is clearly unveiled. The work holds an imbued hue which clings to the world long after the poet's own physical presence has departed. The poems are too *of* this world to ever remain long gone *from out* it. The daily activity the poetry proves be propels it into our lives easy as air and hard as stone. The poems represent the rarest of happenings, elevated beyond any transcendent feeling by the matter-of-fact occurrences of their making. In *The Maximus Poems* Charles Olson declares "I believe in religion, not magic or science / I believe in both man and society as religious." Reading Duncan and O'Hara we approach an understanding of Olson's terms not limited by parochial concerns of current political debate or filtered through academic acerbity. Caught up in the vast breach of our mundane separation from things; when it is things themselves we most long to have and hold. We're thrown off guard surprised that poetry might so deeply embrace gossip on one hand, as with O'Hara, yet also clamber after the counter-draw found in Duncan's enchantments which reach back to fantastical occult roots of Imagination's core being. Yet both poets revel in the heady pleasure of bearing witness to lasting realities gracing the page from time immemorial. Each charts an endless exploration which never fails strike readers anew time and again in poem after poem ranking them amongst the Eternal Company.

EPILOGUE
EMERGENT PRACTICE "JOHN CLARKE VOYAGING": DUNCAN'S WORDS IN THE MOUTHS OF CHARLES OLSON & WILLIAM BLAKE

The following "imagined" conversation between Charles Olson and William Blake borrows heartily from many sources which I came across in my reading during the in-real-time composing of the conversation. This includes significant inspiration as well as much heavy lifting from "Creature, Creator, the Creative Will and Gamemanship" by Robert Duncan which appeared in the summer 1989 issue of Blake scholar and poet John Clarke's under recognized yet vital community-driven publication *Intent: letter of talk, thinking, & document.* This as yet uncollected discussion by Duncan is drawn from tape transcriptions made by Pauline Butling Wah of three talks delivered by Duncan on "The Creative Imagination: the Derivation and Projection of a Poetry" in Buffalo during March 1967 as part of a series hosted by the Institute of Further Studies (Fred Wah, Albert Glover, John Clarke, and George Butterick).

Sometime around 2010 I became aware of the sadly now no longer active journal of poetic response *Wild Orchids* edited by then Buffalo doctoral candidates Robert Dewhurst and Sean Reynolds. I was enthralled with the issue of responses by poets to Herman Melville. I reached out by email expressing my enthusiastic appreciation for the project and a few months later heard back from them that the next issue would focus on poets responding to William Blake. They also inquired whether I would be interested in possibly taking part. I jumped at the chance to send something along their way for consideration. Shortly thereafter I determined that I would write a conversation between Olson and Blake, inspired in large part by the memory of my undergraduate final project collaboration for a class on American Literature of the South with my friend Ben Churchill. We had written an "imagined" conversation, taking turns at his typewriter, between novelist William Faulkner and escaped slave-turned-revolutionary Nat Turner. Much of our text came drawn from out my recollections of reading Faulkner's 1950 Nobel Prize Speech, along with several interviews, and Ben's thorough immersion into the Nat Turner presented by William Styron's *Confessions of Nat Turner.* We received an enthusiastic A and enjoyed brief accolades from professors Kevin Harvey and Don Melander who co-taught the course.

I was excited at the prospect of revisiting such creative immersion into historical literary figures. I knew there was more than enough correspondence of ideas regarding the vitality of the imagination to stimulate an interesting dialogue which would hopelessly mix material from books by and about Olson and Blake along with a few "imaginary" statements. The trick was just to get the ball rolling. As John Clarke had written his doctorate on Blake and thereafter arrived in Buffalo to become heavily influenced by Olson, his work was immediately an inspiration as well. I had never chanced to come across an issue of Clarke's newsletter *Intent* yet at the very moment I was pondering when and how to begin writing the Olson-Blake conversation I happened to get a hold of the summer 1989 issue with transcription of Duncan's previously mentioned talk.

I found myself immediately inspired as I began reading through the issue with a particular eye focused upon Duncan's remarks. (The photo of an extra-large pot-bellied orangutan cooling off with a small towel atop his head framed on one page by Duncan's words only heightened the delight of my engaged reading.) The clarity of his argument's presentation in both comprehension and compression manages a mesmerizing conveyance of poetic speech which thrills and centers the attention. In Clarke's words, Duncan represents a figure of the poet "for whose voice of sanity we have no equivalent." The resulting dialogue is an ever quick and aware example of *reading writing / writing reading.* Over the span of the six or so hours I spent taking down what the respective emanations of Olson and Blake said to one another, a steady pile of books accrued about the table. The voices in the room and from off the page gathered round forming a like chorus of balanced mastery I was honored to witness and record.

JOHN CLARKE VOYAGING

("picking up messages" between anxious emanations Charles Olson and William Blake "recognition of the responsibilities we have as creatures in the garden")

Well, it's not a conspiracy theory. That's Jack Clarke's world.
            Duncan McNaughton

The universe is simple in its own occasion, but that occasion is not completely ours; ours is complex, comprised of subject and object worlds, and the (meaningful) ways these intersect and collide, fold and unfold. The idea in poeticizing the life's inherent complexities is to produce an increasing comprehension of the world as an interlocked sequence of seed beds.
            Stephen Ellis

Olson's report of the meeting, as someone later told me, was that he dug my pants, the material they were made of, and the way I was sitting with my legs crossed.
            John Clarke

Actually, and this is such a divertissement; head lice and crabs are from the same species of louse and due to the slight discord in their mutual genome evolutionary scientists believe they can estimate the time period when humans began to shed body hair and thus maintain two distinctly hairy regions of the body—the head and the pubis. So, for a louse, the distance between the head and groin is vast and was only achievable with a hisuit land bridge that could sustain an expeditionary team of lice with less prodigious grazing across the belly, chest and back, yet still those sparse plainslands provided enough meager viands to complete the harrowing journey. Once the land bridge closed due to our relative hairlessness, (much like the Berring Land Bridge that enabled our

migration from Eastern Siberia into Alaska during the
Pleistocene era) the two sets of lice were now able to let
the driver of evolution, mutation, propel them into their
differences, ie, their distinct adaptations that making
the head louse efficient at parasitism in the drier sparser
climes of the head, and crabs better adept to handle the
lush, tropical ecosystem of the human equator.
W.B. Churchill III

... a continuing projective event of community, the voice
not of a single person (or even mythic persona), but of a
world, itself revealed in a clamor of relations.
Michael Boughn

[*A bare room sparsely set with two chairs and a table or so.
Warm light... William Blake is sitting comfortably with legs
crossed while Olson is hunched forward, eyes beaming, hands
on his knees*]

William Blake   When I am working, writing or
sketching, burning lines and figures from out the plates,
etching the copper...

Charles Olson   *[eagerly]* Yes. Yes! ...

Blake   ...the other, that is Outer, Form is moving
the lines. Words or images,... Color... shapes...shadow...

Olson   *[stammering]* For... only... by

Blake   ...the particular moment is no more lasting
than not.

Olson   In the immediacy of knowing. As the body

forms take/takes its toll. I have known men who never could escape the hinges of their own mind's architecture. You, & nothing less than, *that* is Form itself.

[Gets up and moves about the space. Frequently turning and shooting sharp glances at Blake]

The Only Law: That which IS *is* MATTER.

Blake   They say I'm talking of Angels misunderstanding me. That it may perhaps be that the Angels are misspeaking of me never seems to occur to them. I have swum galactic circumnavigations, exploring the limits that will not do in order to expand further what the eye fails see. & there is no madness, only Vision unadorned by way of complicity such as Science offers. *[Blake speaks with calm yet enthused assuredness.]*

Olson   *[gesturing enthusiastically]* Shards of eternal hours turn up daily amid the wash of the local bay. Garbage of interstellar linearity. I have stood to speak of such matters and others with like-minded Xtians… that only stars state the feeling it is to so stand.

Blake   Eternal forms of our true outer shells connect and communicate together, an entirety of colossal swirl set in motion before any prior action. We are Opposites when truly we most attract.

Olson   *[returning to his seat]* It is my understanding that to not understand one must take the initial step back. To witness, state the thing—fact of—clarity we're grasping towards when first we raise our fist, open the lips to speak.

The Fact of: I am. That universal instant of being nothing further than the words as they form: a becoming of first responses.

Blake   Every composition sleeps when ripeness fails fall to the page. Sky darkens, flames begin leap. Holed up—eyes of the hands guided from without immediate surrounds. Beyond these walls universal want rushes, right now, throughout All. From on high, this have I witnessed by Vision and Sight.

Olson   *[speaking with slow deliberation, almost plodding along]*...and I who never would of questioned, had the nerve, then did, finding out, DID... did ask. Ever since then, all is changed, changing ... newly forced out, alters *Everything* which came before.

Blake   *[with conviction]* ....to bring down those who would wreak vengeance upon the innocent.

Olson   We're creatures, after all. Creatures creating—who must defend against the proposition that one could always be a fraud: The absurdity of that realization! To have it come amid the weavings unweaving this very life ... one is always part of.

Blake   That remembrance forgets forgets best with perfection of a child's perception, the web of who, what, why, when and where. There is no direct link. Only You, standing where you are in place and time, glimpse of vision from where out you gaze. Simple as that.

Olson   A poetry, if that is—as we are acknowledging, if we are—thus concerned with this business, is it? Indeed, that it is a business!

I am struck with wonder at times... how we might say it is all animal, isn't it? ...GEE... I feel as if I'm prowling through my own words, excited and even misunderstood perhaps... all I ask, asking... that is, I might remain open, ...finally, it seems safe to say, is it necessary?

& here, I am I believe quoting, "why are we haunted by Forms? Every man in his proposition" ...by... A poetry? (to bring me back *round*, as it were

Blake   To understand the word whereby one gets to the world as a journey is through rhetorical practice, which is the medium of analogy, itself. This means of now known conceptual locomotion which creates the key potential interplay between disparate and seemingly incommensurable domains....desirous language no matter the overall potential strength for rejuvenation—decisively lacks that Will itself, of which...

Olson   [*a rising whisper*]...by way of necessity...

Blake   ...words of their own accord announcing the freshly hammered out language of their own time in time find way.

Olson   Freedom is the act of creation. Being free you recognize who, where, you are, as against *when* bound— all the things which bind you: habits and such... having to do anything is an evil. Nothing or nobody—[*raising hands up, whooping*] Nobodaddy, hah!—has such a right to so—the freeing as opposed to the ordering, of that: *Will*, I suppose it is.

Blake   [*gesturing for emphasis*] The absolute worst use of energy is that which speculates over what is or is not already present prior to having one's own vision of it. I haven't *become* but only what I've already *been*: to have it said in order, by order, to make it what it already *is* is the lie. That primary equality itself negates by way of necessary contempt for what is defined as being present, by insistent demand that it be the only viable availability, grown out of misapprehension of and by such acts and oaths as past declarations provide. World gone wrong in presuppositions based on ill favor in face of the both ever present and eternal now, having been so blinded by those few in charge of Power, thus it follows...

Olson   To have been alive, even now! to that Always of which you refer, the said reference to the fact of such idea. One stands on the side of the good not that the good win but that there be good.

Blake   Some imbalances are necessary, being Just. One stands against many to benefit all on behalf of immediate few. To acknowledge that surrounding whole—those *pure* objects of contemplation, the stars in their courses, history in glowing dust flowing in the blood. That which first led Man astray in wonder leads us back again when writing.

Olson   [*slowly rises and moves about, gesturing and posturing his way*] The measure of a New World must of necessity be conjured, that is to say, procured, from out the depths of the celestial—both above & below—so, from out the ocean, that is, as alike simultaneously of the stars above— as, say, is cryptically the case mentioned here and there through the historical record as preserved to this day in India, Persia, elsewhere... not accidentally rather decidedly...

That the order of the Dead is the order of Things... Between the Image and the Poet lies the Poem—that very vehicle by which the two enter the world as indivisible...

Blake   [*eyes transfixed off above Olson's shoulder, self-mesmerized*] Was it yesterday the great Painted Bird came to call? & such a bird! He perched at the top of the enormous Poison Tree as I was in the garden and frequently glanced down at me—a living emblem of my Visions. How I pitied him as I envisioned his limited sight when compared to my own—yet how he sang and danced while cocking his fierce head and taking it all in.

[*as if awakened*] My Vision reflected back upon me, so true.

Olson   [*still up and moving about*] Considering what a bodacious (here I do 'learn' from out younger mouths— borrowing when and wherever as I do) number of millennia human folks have spent instructing plants and animals, it's weird to entertain such a lot of ancient experiences... the vast differences of approach, in the end, becomes much like a carnival outlasting a metropolis.

The gods appeared and disappeared in the fields—what of the role cities now play?

Blake   The other day as I sat among a group of

Immortals, I asked one if she had ever seen any humans capable of becoming something else during the period of her enduring tenure. She replied that she had not, however she had recently been following the path left by a set of human footprints and witnessed them transform to regular old rail tracks embedded in decades-old asphalt and that she had later met the individual to whom the particular footprints belonged. She related that the conversation was marvelous.

Olson   [*nearly leaping about, as if to take flight*] Like what it means to "stand by one's word", & how to do it! Really, I mean how... do... you... are you... is it possible to stand when the page is so bare as to no longer be a page! The loss of the physical, Ka-Chunk! This damn technological advancement... of the digital... where is it headed... I've no idea, in fact I doubt any DO!

The enemy—& typically so!—is as banal as the local realtor and as dull as short term planning for profit has proven itself—

Blake   An answer to present misalignments within the power structure is the restoration of the individual to her own role based upon her identity within, and towards, that of community as well as economy. This is a matter of the spirit being uncontested—the soul, our ultimate Form being that of sharing an ethereal nature while simultaneously and substantially rooted in earthly matters.

So Power must, in its proper role as promoter and presenter of peace and general welfare of all, step up and crush rather than collude with unjust practices. A nation, after all, is composed thereby, its heads of government intending to stand between and regulate wealth—corporations, "special interests" & such—and Power, that is, itself—is of that nature so granted by choice of its constituents. All else is miserable truth.

Olson ... any so-called universalizing of Western liberal democracy as a final form of human government is such utter bullshit ...

[*sitting back down, hunching forward, eyes beaming at Blake*]

The "ten thousand things" are *of* both "heaven and earth" & I find myself assuring my self that by "earth" is meant far more than one quarter of a hemisphere! Putting thought into print is one thing, encouraging a mass migratory shifting of consciousness into that of a global totality, or else— is something of quite another order! That whole mess of message left me behind long ago—it ain't the wild guys who do the killing.

To be alive in the poetic sense is to live in absolute opposition to death, your own & others. The danger is two-fold and aligns, on both sides, right atop the fact of it being "a difference of use of the system." Because "use" of any "system" is what we're fighting against... to have it—be it "Power" or whatever—spurning itself out, the rhythmic deferral of substance refusing grasping hands of corruption.

Blake [*Voice rising, insistent*] A doom-full prophecy: Final Hours. To be an error & cast out: those who sought control and were engulfed.

While it being true I am a very contrary fellow, I do not

take such stance lightly, I strike out to see that what may be is not merely what is. Not just a species of the arbitrary, rather yet an engagement with the supposition underlying, analogy as *coincidence* is one towards which I feel compelled address. Abandoned to the fury of symbols, how else imagine the mind's greatest adventure than as a series of sorts to the paradise of pitfalls?

Olson   [*offhandedly*] Like what are poets for? I give you the end of a golden string with the flurry of the day's business obviously freed— shitting in the wind ... this is no night of Gloucester Revelations!

Although, that is, self-correcting as I do, the past doesn't mean anything 'cept to those alive & still observing—as I say, what is meant by seeing for one's self, 'istorin—in the present, immediacy of Now. You only speak yourself through one life at a time, remember that. Make it count.

Blake   Like foreign substances infiltrating the blood-stream, a beginning loss of reason with right Reason aligned; Nowhere near Europe's, i.e. The West's, nightmarish pact, "exterminate all the brutes," is simply jabbering nonsense. The brutes are those "leading," if there are any at all. If we now could literally bury the hatchet, instead of that part of the brain that's afraid it might only like to use one, we'd discover there is such a thing as "secret sharer"

Olson   [*surprised, eyes widening, mouth open*] The making of how many poems equals a home?

BIBLIOGRAPHY

Clarke, John, ed. *Intent. Letter of Talk, Thinking, & Document.* Vol. 1, no. 2 Summer 1989

Collis, Stephen and Lyons, Graham, ed. *Reading Duncan Reading: Robert Duncan and the Poetics of Derivation* (University of Iowa Press 2012)

Katz, Daniel. *The Poetry of Jack Spicer* (Edinburgh University Press 2008)

Duncan, Michael and Wagstaff, Christopher, ed. *An Opening of the Field: Jess, Robert Duncan, and Their Circle* (Pomegranate Communications 2013)

Duncan, Robert. *The Collected Early Poems and Plays* edited and with an introduction by Peter Quartermain (University of California Press 2012)

—————. *The Collected Essays and Other prose* edited and with an introduction by James Maynard (University of California Press 2014)

—————. *The Collected Later Poems and Plays* edited and with an introduction by Peter Quartermain (University of California Press 2014)

—————. *The H.D. Book* edited and with an introduction by Michael Boughn and Victor Coleman (University of California Press 2011)

—————. *A poet's mind: collected interviews with Robert*

Duncan, 1960-1985 edited by Christopher Wagstaff with a foreword by Gerrit Lansing (North Atlantic Books 2012)

Hampson, Robert and Montgomery, Will, ed. *Frank O'Hara now: new essays on the New York Poet* (University of Liverpool Press 2011)

Jarnot, Lisa. *Robert Duncan: the Ambassador from Venus* (University of California Press 2012)

Jess. *Jess : o! tricky cad & other Jessoterica* edited by Michael Duncan (Siglio Press 2012)

Maynard, James, ed. *Re:) working the ground : essays on the late writings of Robert Duncan* (Palgrave Macmillan 2011)

Nichols, Miriam, ed. *The Astonishment Tapes: Talks on Poetry and Autobiography with Robin Blaser and Friends* (University of Alabama Press 2015)

Rumaker, Michael. *Robert Duncan in San Francisco* with an interview & letters edited by Ammiel Alcalay and Megan Paslawski (City Lights Publishers 2013)

Vincent, John Emil, ed. *After Spicer: Critical Essays* (Wesleyan University Press 2011)

Ackowledgements

I am in lasting debt to the authors, editors, and publishers of the works (see Bibliography) quoted from and discussed throughout this essay. Without their efforts of seeing the publications into existence my own words in response would not exist. I thank them all for contributing to the lasting recognition of Robert Duncan's life and work as well as that of his associates.

Each chapter of *The Duncan Era* contains at least some material originally written as a book review essay, and in some cases two pieces originally published separately have been here joined together. I am ever grateful to the venues which provided a forum on-line and/or in print for initial publication: *Bookslut* (Chapters One, Three, Four, and Six), *Entropy* (Chapter One), *Jacket2* (Chapter Seven), *Rain Taxi* (Chapters Two, Five, and Six), *Your Impossible Voice* (Chapter Two), and *Wild Orchids* (Epilogue). Working with the editors involved has been a pleasure. I truly appreciate their support and editorial advisement.

Lastly, I wish acknowledge that this writing, as is the case with all my work, is inextricably meshed within many hours of conversation with innumerable friends and associates. My participation in the conversation began in the fall of 1998 when I enrolled in the Poetics Program at the now defunct New College of California in San Francisco. It has never been lost on me that the Poetics program was in many ways originally established in part to give Robert Duncan a place to teach. In my personal experience, his Spirit never left the program. This book is in part a tribute to the subsequent abundant years of generous walks drinks & talks which all began there. Cheers.

PATRICK JAMES DUNAGAN lives in San Francisco and works at Gleeson Library for the University of San Francisco. A graduate of the Poetics program from the now-defunct New College of California he's currently helping to edit an anthology of critical writings by Poetics program alumni and faculty. He also edited and wrote the introduction for poet Owen Hill's *A Walk Among the Bogus* (Lavender Ink). His essays and book reviews appear frequently with a wide number of both online and print publications. His most recent books include: *"There are people who think that painters shouldn't talk": A Gustonbook* (Post Apollo), *Das Gedichtete* (Ugly Duckling), and *from Book of Kings* (Bird and Beckett Books).